Kingdom Communion

Mystery of the Fourth Cup

Stan Newton

Kingdom Communion

Mystery of the Fourth Cup

Dr. Stan Newton

Copyright © Dr. Stan Newton

ISBN 978-1-61529-182-3

Vision Publishing
1115 D Street
Ramona, CA 92065
1-800-9-VISION
www.booksbyvision.org

Endorsements

It is always a delight to read the work of a practical thinker. Dr Stan Newton always stimulates my thinking, and does so in a strong theological and practical ministry sense. In his latest book, Kingdom Communion, Stan unpacks for us the historical and modern day views and usages of the Eucharist, bringing a fresh visitation on this most important doctrine in scripture. As my dear friend, theologian Dr. Ken Chant reminded me, in the New Testament there is only one piece of furniture mentioned related to worship…not a pulpit, no sound system, not one offering plate, not even comfortable chairs to sit in…just a table…the Table of the Lord, were we either weekly or weakly renew our covenant with the Lord, providing strength and health for our journey. Unlike most books on Communion, Kingdom Communion is filled with strong theology and practical illustration, thus making it a source of great help in preaching Communion services, and for deepening one's knowledge of this important, vital doctrine.

Dr. Stan E. DeKoven
President
Vision International University

Stan Newton has written a useful book. That word, useful, is appropriate because this book will serve you. The topic of Communion is about worship. Most problems faced in the world are, at their core, worship problems. How often should we receive communion? How should we go about it? Why should we take part in the Lord's Supper? Newton answers difficult questions inviting those who read to partake of who Jesus is. Revealed in his life, death and resurrection, Jesus is the substance of all things hoped for.

What did Peter learn at the foot washing in the upper room? He found out that it is not in the acknowledgement of need that makes Jesus king. What matters is receiving him as he is. As children, we learn that we are what we eat, so eat, drink and remember. It's a practice worth repeating.

Scott Crowder
Senior Leader of DreamHouse Church
Newport News, VA
JesusLoves757.com

It's God's desire that a greater revelation of His love and power in the new covenant be understood by His church. For too long, we have had such a limited view of God and His kingdom because of the traditions of teaching in the church, but this is changing.

Dr. Stan Newton's book on Kingdom Communion will take you into a deeper understanding of the new covenant, the kingdom of God, and our co-heir marriage to Jesus the King. There is still so much to be explored concerning the new covenant kingdom of God, and this New Jerusalem made up of believers all over the world, the Wife of Jesus.

Paul prayed that believers would have "the spirit of revelation". In other words, Paul prayed that we all would have understanding concerning many things Jesus has done for us in the Spirit, this Kingdom Communion. Stan's book is another piece of this ongoing revelation that God is releasing to His church today.

Dr. Stan Newton's book will challenge the traditional ideas concerning "communion" in the Body of Christ.

David Duncan
Author and Teacher

Table of Contents

Chapter 1

Dynamic Communion

Communion is a kingdom feast. Communion is a renewal of the new covenant. Communion is when the church experiences the dynamic presence of Christ. Communion is a demonstration of church unity. Communion is the experience of the fourth cup. Yet, from my travels and study, few of these truths are being embraced by the average church. We explain communion in many ways, and for the most part, celebration of the King and his covenant are not one of them. This cannot be ignored any longer. The Evangelical Church needs a major overall of its understanding and experience of the Lord's Supper. We have lost its connection to the new covenant and to the kingdom. As we grow in the revelation of God's ever-increasing kingdom our experience of the Lord's Table must follow suit.

Kingdom Communion is written with the conviction we are missing a glorious opportunity. If we continually see communion as 'not that important' our worship services will fail to make the kingdom transition God is searching for. A revelation of Christ and his advancing kingdom affects every doctrine and this includes the Lord's Supper. Over several decades, we have enjoyed a rebirth of lively spontaneous worship. We have heard the prophetic voice return to the church. There has been a great flow of spiritual gifts and miracles. This journey has been a great adventure. Yet, we have also paid a price. Our purely emotional worship is taking a toll. It becomes difficult to maintain the level of emotion needed to bring the same level of excitement week after week. Many believers are drained and they are not sure why. This is especially true in Pentecostal/Charismatic churches. What is missing? We have neglected to add biblical objectivity into our worship services. We need a balance. Yes, we must have the presence of the Holy Spirit in our services, which moves our emotions. We also need intellectual worship, or a worship which affirms and challenges our thinking. Bringing back the Lord's Table as part of our Christian worship will establish the balance we need. This is no small matter; the future existence of many local churches is at stake. Emotional worship which lacks objectivity creates an overly emotional congregation without the qualities of stability and perseverance. Over time these types of churches implode within themselves.

Kingdom Communion draws the best from historic perspectives. We are not 'haters of history' nor haphazardly swipe away Christian traditions. Yet, we are convinced the full story is untold. We want more. We desire more of the reality of communion and less of its ritualistic elements. We want more than a slice of dry bread; we want to feed on the living Christ. We want more than a sip of wine; we want the anointing of the Spirit. We want more than 'faith,' we want the thing faith longs for. We want more than a 'mystery,' we want to know the 'man behind the curtain.' We want more than a memory of Jesus, we want Jesus. This is a tall order. Yet, as we examine Kingdom Communion a window of understanding will be opened.

It is not that we have abandoned communion, but we have downgraded it to the bottom of our priority list. Communion has lost its luster. A variety of reasons are given. Our time is limited on Sundays. We are moving away from church rituals. A few advocate that communion is not necessary under the new covenant. It makes visitors and even church members uncomfortable (no one wants to be damned for partaking unworthily). As there are many reasons for not partaking communion there are more reasons to take it.

Jesus left us few direct commands. Two of these are "making disciples of all nations" and "do this in remembrance of me." And it is these two we have difficulty with. Churches get involved with numerous things and place responsibility for world missions on the back burner. We avoid communion for who knows what reason. There are so many reasons, shall we say excuses, for not doing what we are told.

One of the words I have chosen to use express the communion is 'dynamic'. In most cases our standard communion services are anything but dynamic. This expresses what is missing in partaking of the Lord's Table. When words like, solemn, introspective, repentance and ritualistic describe our time at the Table, we need change. Dynamic is the direction we need to go.

According to the Merriam-Webster dictionary dynamic means, "always active or changing" and "having or showing a lot of energy." The presence of God experienced by the church in the communion is certainly active and manifests the energy of God. The format may be the same, the Scriptures read may be the same, the bread and wine may be the same, but the presence of God, the real presence of Jesus is never the same. Jesus never changes but how we experience him is constantly changing. Christians who feel communion is boring are too focused on the mechanics and not the reality of what is happening. Touching God is never boring. God touching us is always transforming.

Experiencing Christ in the communion does not have to be an over the top emotional encounter. When we look to our emotions or the outward excitement level to evaluate the truthfulness of our experience, we give in to 'emotional blackmail.' We may feel nothing. We may not receive a great revelation. Yet, the quiet strong presence of Christ is among us, strengthening and nourishing us. No wonder our churches are weak and filled with drama queens (and kings). People come to church for their emotional sugar high and are not feeding from the Table of the Lord. It is called the Lord's Table for a purpose, we are to eat, not physical food, but the substance from heaven.

This book has a single theme. My hope is to move the church towards a greater appreciation of communion, and to grasp the significance of the relationship between communion and the kingdom of God. The reality of the new covenant to oversee our position on communion is essential. This will prove to be most difficult. During years of being in church fellowships, I have found great apathy towards communion. Nevertheless, the challenge is worthwhile.

Christians are wanting more from church and leaders are finding it difficult to figure out exactly what they want. By understanding and embracing Kingdom communion the Spirit-filled church can rebuild its faulty foundations. We can build spiritually stable people. This can be done without losing our edge; the powerful presence and gifts of the Holy Spirit. One does not exclude the other. They are mutually supportive.

What Difference Does It Make?

The primary reason Christians change church membership to a Pentecostal/Charismatic church is their desire for spiritual experiences. Their previous church may have preached the word, kept the ordinances, and stood unwaveringly for truth; yet offered little hope of 'experiencing the Spirit.' Attending church where the service is the same year after year was no longer desired and many voted with their feet. During the early years of the Charismatic movement, in the late 60's and 70's, it was common to remain in your traditional church and testify to your 'Spirit-filled' experience. As the years went by these Spirit-filled believers realized their churches and denominations were not changing and probably never would, so they left for greener pastures. It was during these years' non-denominational, independent charismatic churches exploded across the landscape. Finally, these Spirit-filled believers have a place to grow, to experience the new things of God and his family. And for multitudes of people it worked. They found the church of their dreams and they joyfully jumped in. Now, years later, things are not working as well. We stand and clap to modern music, at times we sing, but mostly just listen to the worship team. The Pastor proclaims better days are coming and prophesizes a great revival. Or the opposite, we are told the world is heading towards destruction and the antichrist is secretly organizing his takeover. Sure, there are churches where the 'newness' of the work of the Spirit and his mighty presence is more real than before, but for many churches, something is missing and everyone knows it.

When a movement begins to die, there are more questions than answers. Who is to blame? Where did we miss God? Were we building upon faulty foundations? I also have questions. Why do many apostolic networks explode on the scene, grow rapidly, enjoy great influence, and then around the 20-25-year mark, implode? This is wavering slightly from the single theme, but as the Lord's Table is restored to its proper place it will help Charismatic churches become a stalwart and faithful witnesses to the truth. It is hoped that in 200 years, people can point to a Charismatic church in their community and say, "This church has been a blessing to our city for several centuries." Longevity is a characteristic missing in many churches. By embracing kingdom eschatology, new covenant truth and restoring the Lord's Table, we can change the 'church here-gone tomorrow' reality. This restoration will greatly assist us by adding 'objective worship' back into our largely subjective, experience seeking services.

There is a theological movement which is injecting new life in the church. The failures of modern Evangelical eschatology (with its 'rapture' focused and escapist mentality) are being exposed for their misuse of Scripture. An eschatology centering on the reign of Christ and his advancing kingdom is replacing the doom and gloom pop theology. Alongside our increased understanding of the Kingdom of God a revolution in how we see and apply the new covenant is exploding on the Christian world. With our new appreciation of kingdom and covenant, it is time to reclaim the Lord's Table as central in our Sunday worship services.

Chapter 2

History and Traditions

Are we affected by our history and tradition? The best way not to be controlled by past events is to understand them. Knowing how the church viewed the Lord's Supper over the centuries will bring perspective to how we should practice it. We begin with a brief review of how the Lord's Table is seen in the major denominations of the church. They can be grouped in five major positions; Transubstantiation (Roman Catholic), Divine Mystery (Eastern Orthodox), Consubstantiation (Lutheran), Real Presence (Reformed) and Memorialism (Evangelical). Added to this menu is a sixth view which is non-traditional; which is 'Spiritual Communion." The hundreds of Christian denominations normally fall within one of these positions. After we examine these models of communion I will offer my position of Kingdom Communion- the dynamic presence of Christ and what it means to partake of the fourth cup.

Before reviewing the historical positions on communion, we should first know why we have so many different names for a single event. We have, breaking bread, communion, The Lord's Supper, Eucharist, Mass, and the Lord's Table. All of them derive from a mix of history, tradition and (hopefully) Scripture. Each name is used to emphasis a certain aspect of the event.

Breaking of Bread

In the early church the name used to celebrate what Jesus began was simply 'breaking of bread' (Acts 2:42). This was more than the ordinarily bread breaking as in the daily family meal but was 'special,' it was breaking bread with members of the church.

Communion

The second common name is communion. It comes from the phrase 'the sharing' which is English, from the Greek word, 'koinōnia'. It can also be translated 'communion.' This sharing with one another or communion with Jesus and his people is special, so churches often add the name 'holy' to communion.[1]

The Lord's Supper

The term 'The Lord's Supper' comes simply from the fact that it was evening when Jesus and his disciples first learned of this new way of doing Passover. As a child, I grew up having breakfast, lunch, and supper. The word supper is seldom used now, being replaced with dinner. Calling the meal 'Supper' has little theological meaning but possibly has emotional ties to the past where families would gather in the evening to share their meal. Many families have lost the value of eating together in the evening so coming to church for a 'supper'; even if it only a cracker and juice, produces good feelings.

Eucharist

N.T. Wright provides a good understanding of the word Eucharist. "Jesus always said 'thank you' to God; the church, in breaking the bread and pouring out the wine said, 'thank you' to God for what he did in Jesus. The Greek for 'thank you' is euchaisto...and some of the earliest Christians therefore called the meal 'the Eucharist.'[2] What seems like an official word is just Greek for saying thanks or the thanksgiving we give to God.

Mass

After a few hundred years of Christian history another term became popular. When the saints finished the bread and wine the

[1] Tom Wright, The Meal Jesus gave Us, Westminster John Know Press, Louisville-London, 1999, p. 35-36
[2] Ibid.

person presiding would say, "Go-you are sent out." N.T Wright, "The Latin for this phrase is 'ite-missa Est'. From there developed the word 'Mass' the meal that ends with this sending-out, this commissioning."[3] Today we equate 'Mass' with the Roman Catholic tradition and think of it as a 'sacrifice' more than a commissioning.

The Lord's Table

The term often used in churches and one I like is the 'Lord's Table.' It reminds us of the purpose for eating this meal together. We are feeding not on human substance but that which is in Jesus. We are feeding on the presence and body of Jesus. It is Jesus who invites us to his meal. He has set the table and provides us with the best food available; the food of heaven.

There is meaning in the various names. I prefer 'Communion' and the 'Lord's Table' and use them interchangeably. We must remember it is the table of the Lord and we come to 'commune' with him and with each other.

Theological Views

As there are different names there are also differing theological positions on Communion. We now review six different views held by Christians on the meaning of 'breaking bread.'

Transubstantiation

The official position of the Roman Catholic Church is called transubstantiation. This act of receiving the Lord's Supper or "Mass" is central to their faith. If Evangelical's have undervalued communion, Roman Catholicism has done the opposite in their doctrine of transubstantiation. When the Priest lifts the elements and prays over them, it is believed that the bread and wine turn into the 'physical' body and blood of Jesus. In the Roman Catholic

---

[3] Ibid.

tradition, preaching or singing is not the heart of worship, receiving the Eucharist is. From an article published in 'The American Catholic (an on-line source for Catholic theology and culture) it says "Catholics believe the Eucharist, or Communion, is both a sacrifice and a meal. We believe in the real presence of Jesus, who died for our sins. As we receive Christ's Body and Blood, we also are nourished spiritually and brought closer to God."[4] Roman Catholics believe communion is both a 'sacrifice' and a 'meal.' It is one of their seven sacraments. "The Latin word *sacramentum* means "a sign of the sacred." The seven sacraments are ceremonies that point to what is sacred, and therefore, important for Christians. They are special occasions for experiencing God's saving presence. That's what theologians mean when they say that sacraments are at the same time signs and instruments of God's grace."[5]

Several important points in these statements help to distinguish the view of the Roman Catholic Church from most Protestants. First, Protestants do not believe that partaking of communion is a 'sacrifice.' The death of Jesus on the cross was a "once for all" sacrifice (Heb. 10:12). No other means, no other 'sacrifice' can remove sin. Second, Roman Catholics teach receiving the Eucharist is "experiencing God's saving grace." Does communion supply grace to the believer? Absolutely! I believe it does. Does it provide 'saving grace?" No! We are saved by the death of Jesus who died 2,000 years ago.

Even though we disagree with the theology of transubstantiation with its real sacrifice, the practice in many Evangelical Churches has a similar attitude with its strong focus on sin and suffering. Thus, communion is rather a solemn experience.

---

[4] American Catholic, americancatholic.org
[5] Ibid.

Divine Liturgy or Mystery (Eastern Orthodox)

What is the view of the Eastern Orthodox Church on communion? Many Evangelicals think it is exactly akin to the Roman Catholic view, and they are partially correct, but miss an important distinction. From the Greek Orthodox Archdiocese of America, "Earthly Ministry, Death, Resurrection and Ascension in Glory, is a historical event which unites eternity and creation. This insight of biblical realism is captured in the elaborate and highly symbolical worship of the Orthodox Church. Easter is the "Feast of Feasts", repeated annually and weekly in Sunday worship. The Church celebrates and participates in the event of the Resurrection of the Lord at each Divine Liturgy. Each moment of Christ's life and ministry is seen in the Light of the Resurrection. Each worship motif of the Church is intimately related to the Proclamation and participation in this saving event. Every aspect of liturgy and prayer is understood as an effort at the beautiful expression of this reality. All the senses are employed in Orthodox worship. Every appropriate means is employed to reveal in human terms the mystery of God's love for us. The Holy Eucharist, known as the Divine Liturgy, is the chief worship service and is celebrated on all Sundays and Holy days during the liturgical year. Orthodoxy maintains a high sacramental view. The Sacraments are visible signs of an invisible Divine Grace. The elements of bread and wine in the Holy Eucharist are believed to be the very Body and Blood of Jesus Christ received for the remission of sins and life everlasting."[6]

Although a single name is not used to describe the Lord's Supper it is often referred to as the 'Divine Liturgy or Divine Mystery.'

Both Eastern (Greek) Orthodox and Roman Catholic's hold to physical presence. Although Roman Catholic's use the word

---

[6] Greek Orthodox Archdiocese of America, www.goarch.org

"real" and the Orthodox use "the very" body and blood of Jesus, in essence, it is the same. Once we move beyond the issue of presence, the actual practice of communion reflects two different works of Christ. Sacrifice is the big issue for Roman Catholic's, it is seen as a real death of Jesus whereas the Orthodox see communion as a celebration of the resurrection of Jesus. There is truth in the 'resurrection centered' view of Eastern Orthodox Church. We can build from this starting point. It brings us nearer to 'kingdom communion' where Jesus is celebrated as King, of which, the resurrection was the first step to his enthronement.

The Orthodox prayer recited before receiving the elements contains much of their theology

I believe, O Lord, and I confess that Thou art truly the Christ, the Son of the Living God, who camest into the world to save sinners, of whom I am the first (see 1 Tim 1:15).

I believe also that this is truly Thine own most pure Body, and that this is truly Thine own most precious Blood. Therefore I pray Thee: Have mercy upon me and forgive me my transgressions, committed in word and deed, whether consciously or unconsciously.

And make me worthy to partake without condemnation of Thy most pure Mysteries, for the remission of sins and unto life everlasting.

Of Thy Mystical Supper, O Son of God, accept me today as a communicant. For I will not speak of Thy Mystery to Thine enemies, neither like Judas will I give Thee a kiss; but like the thief will I confess Thee: "Remember me, O Lord, in Thy Kingdom."

May the communion of Thy Holy Mysteries be neither to my judgment, nor to my condemnation, 0 Lord, but to the healing of soul and body. [7]

Unlike other traditions including most Protestants, the Orthodox faithful receive Holy Communion on a spoon. They are given both the consecrated bread (NIKA) and the sanctified wine. All members who are prepared including small children and infants partake of Holy Communion. "Jesus has told us, it is "not of this world." The Eucharist, because it belongs to God's Kingdom, is truly free from the earth-born "logic" of fallen humanity. From John of Damascus: "If you enquire how this happens, it is enough for you to learn that it is through the Holy Spirit ... we know nothing more than this, that the word of God is true, active, and omnipotent, but in its manner of operation unsearchable."[8]

We must look at each tradition and see if anything can be kept. I like the 'resurrection centered' approach. I also like that they do not deny children access to the Table. On the negative side, I am not in favor of 'hoping' you are worthy to partake. It seems very introspective and too similar to the standard Evangelical approach. The Orthodox Church concentrates on the living Christ. I find this aspect both theologically sound and good practice.

Consubstantiation (Lutheranism)

Unless you are a Lutheran you probably cannot give a simple definition of how they view communion. We think if fits somewhere in the middle between Roman Catholic and the standard Evangelical view, but beyond this, we are not sure. The official term of the Lutheran view is consubstantiation (although Martin Luther never used the word). It means in receiving communion the bread and wine does not change into the 'physical presence' of Christ yet his presence is still within the elements. "This view was proposed by Martin Luther in response to the

---

[7] Orthodoxwiki, http://orthodoxwiki.org
[8] Ibid.

views of the Catholic Church on Communion. He stated that the bread and wine do not change into the actual body and blood of Jesus as Catholics held, but rather, Christ's body and blood are present "in, with, and under" the elements. He explained this using the analogy that in the same way heat is present in a piece of hot iron, so Christ is present in the elements."[9]

Luther saw in the Roman Catholic view an over literal understanding of how bread and wine become the physical presence of Christ. "What Luther argued was not that transubstantiation was wrong but that trying to explain how the bread and wine are the body and blood of Christ is a human mistake. For Luther, the mystery of the incarnation is tied directly into the mystery of how the Eucharistic bread and wine are the body and blood of Christ. Luther in his 1528 treatise on the Lord's Supper in fact says, "If you can explain how Christ is both fully God and man I will explain how the bread and wine are his body and blood." For Luther, the elements at the table are both bread and Christ's body."[10]

We cannot take space to fully examine the Lutheran view as there are numerous Lutheran Denominations. Yet, their view of communion is a basic element of their worship which makes them Lutheran. In one sense, they teach the bread and wine are not just mere bread and wine (see below) and yet they desire to separate themselves from the Roman Catholic view. So, they say the real (maybe physical) Christ is somewhere in or around the bread and wine. A local church with the Lutheran Church Missouri Synod states their view on who can receive communion.

"In keeping with the doctrine and practice of our church body, The Lutheran Church - Missouri Synod (LC-MS), we practice a Close Communion. That is, we normally offer Holy Communion only to those with whom we are close in belief. Therefore, we

---

[9] Jesus Alive, www.jesusalive.com
[10] *Grace Lutheran Church, Lutheran Teaching on Holy Communion,* *www.onlinegracelutheran.org*

invite only those who are members of the LC-MS to join us at the Lord's Table. Since it is our strong belief (according to God's Holy Word) that we are partaking more than mere bread and wine, but also Christ's true body and blood, we ask that out of respect for our beliefs that you would refrain from communing at this altar…. All those who hold a confession differing from that of The Lutheran Church-Missouri Synod, and are unable to receive the Sacrament at this time are invited to meditate on God's Word during the distribution and pray for the day when all divisions will have ceased."[11]

If you were a visitor in this Lutheran Church and even though a committed Christian, you are asked to pass the elements and not partake. Only members of their denomination are allowed. At least they are clear. This is called 'closed communion' and other denominations also hold to this rule. The opposite position is 'open communion' which mean 'all Christians' no matter what denomination may partake of communion in their churches.

Lutherans can be applauded for their desire to keep the real presence of Christ in the Table. Their weakness is their insistence, although ambiguous, of maintaining the teaching of a physical presence of Christ somewhere around the elements.

Memorialism (or Zwinglism-Evangelical)

Ulrich Zwingli was a Swiss Reformer. As a city chaplain, he spoke before the Zurich City Council in January 1523. The Protestant Reformation made its way over the Alps from Luther's Germany and Switzerland was next in line to experience reformation. He persuaded the council and received permission to continue his preaching. As a parish Priest, he felt responsible for the people. He wanted to preach the Bible and move away from

---

[11] Richard Boshoven, Trinity Memorial Lutheran Church, www.tmlchurch.com

ecclesiastical tradition. So, he bought a copy of Erasmus's Greek New Testament and preached from it.[12]

"In 1524 he wedded his wife publicly, insisting that pastors had the right to marry. In 1525 he and others convinced the city to abolish the Mass, with its emphasis on the miracle of transubstantiation, and replace it with a simple service that included the Lord's Supper but only as a symbolic memorial."[13]

When Zwingli changed his view of communion he did more than distance himself from the Roman Catholic view, he moved away from Luther. This lead to a meeting with Martin Luther. "At a 1529 meeting at Marburg, called to unite the two movements, Luther and Zwingli met. They agreed on 14 points of doctrine, they stumbled on the fifteenth: the Lord's Supper. Against Zwingli's view, Luther insisted on Christ's literal presence. Zwingli balked. Luther said Zwingli was of the devil and that he was nothing but a wormy nut. Zwingli resented Luther's treating him "like an ass." It was evident no reconciliation was possible.[14]

Those who study Luther know his reputation for having a sharp tongue. And from this point on, the Reformation in Switzerland headed in a different direction. If the meeting had gone better and they had agreed to 'disagree' for a season until a possible statement of unity could have been made, it would have changed the history of the Protestant Reformation.

What was Zwingli's view on the Lord's Table? Today it is called Memorialism. It is simply the view which sees communion as purely symbolic. Most contemporary Evangelical's follow a form of Zwingli's view of communion. The wine (grape juice in America) and bread are symbols of the sacrifice of Jesus on the cross. They help us remember. Beyond being symbols to assist our memory, they serve no purpose. There is no 'physical

---

[12] Christian History, Ulrich Zwingli Militant Swiss Reformer, www.christianhistory.net
[13] Ibid.
[14] Ibid.

presence.' There is no 'mystery' taking place, and there is no 'spiritual presence.' Since Jesus is with us always there can be no added presence during communion.

Evangelicals make a point of introspection before receiving communion. We bow in silent prayer searching our hearts for 'unconfessed sin.' Usually it is an easy search as all sorts of shortcomings are recalled. We are warned not to partake if we have sin, otherwise we are bringing possible damnation into our lives. It is no celebration.

I find the description of an average Evangelical communion service by Steve Atkerson hits close to my experience. "Many modern churches partake of the Lord's Supper with more of a funeral atmosphere. An organ softly plays reflective music. Every head is bowed and every eye is closed as people quietly and introspectively search their souls for unconfessed sin. The cup and loaf are laid out on a small table, covered over by a white cloth, almost like a corpse would be during a funeral. Deacons somberly, like pall bearers, pass out the elements."[15] If visitors in our churches cannot distinguish between a funeral and a communion service we have problems.

The Southern Baptist Convention states their view on communion. "The Lord's Supper is a symbolic act of obedience whereby members ... memorialize the death of the Redeemer and anticipate His second coming."[16] This is a short and concise statement of how most Evangelicals view communion. Their focus is first on obedience, then, on the meaning of communion. We are to 'memorialize' or remember his death. How long should the church observe communion? We are to continue until the second coming of Christ.

The Assemblies of God state their position.

---

[15] Steve Atkerson, The Lord's Supper-A Holy Meal, http://www.ntrf.org
[16] Southern Baptist Convention, www.sbc.net

"The Lord's Supper, consisting of the elements – bread and the fruit of the vine – is the symbol expressing our sharing the divine nature of our Lord Jesus Christ (2 Peter 1:4), a memorial of His suffering and death (1 Corinthians 11:26) and a prophecy of His second coming (1 Corinthians 11:26) and is enjoined on all believers "till He come!"[17]

Being a historic Pentecostal denomination the Assemblies of God add a greater 'spiritual appreciation' to communion. Yet, this sharing in the divine nature does not happen during communion but is a "symbol" of it. Following this their statement is similar to Southern Baptist, concentrating on the suffering and death of Jesus and ends with an eschatological statement. Taking communion is a "prophecy" of the Second Coming.

We have seen the view of Roman Catholic's, Eastern Orthodox, Lutheranism and that of Zwingli. Yet, the reformation on communion was not over, another view soon arrived.

Reformed

The Reformed view of communion takes a position different from Roman Catholicism, their Lutheran reformers and even from Zwingli. From all the various views of the 16th century Calvin makes an on-course correction, which in my view, was needed. He felt Luther's consubstantiation remained too close to the Roman Catholic view and Zwingli's position was overly symbolic. Calvin taught the bread and wine remained bread and wine, there was no physical or mystical change taking place. Yet, there was to be expected a real or spiritual presence in the Lord's Supper. Calvin saw communion as the time when believers in Christ (the church) spiritually entered heaven and were spiritually nourished in the action of receiving the Lord's Table. Those teaching a 'physical' change taught the opposite; Jesus leaves his appointed place at the right hand of the Father in heaven and comes down to earth where

---

[17] Assemblies of God, www.ag.org

he becomes the bread and wine. Because of Calvin's belief that Christ presently reigns from the throne of David in heaven, it was difficult for him to accept Jesus leaving his place of authority at the right hand of the Father. Yet he believed there was a real presence of Christ in the communion.

Calvin resisted reducing the Lord's Supper to mere symbolism. Therefore, Zwingli's view was not acceptable. He also wanted no portion of any physical change taking place in the bread and wine. Therefore, Roman Catholic, Eastern Orthodox and Lutheranism were to be rejected. Taking communion was not a magic trick nor was it mere remembrance; Jesus is with us in Spirit. Therefore, if Jesus is to remain in heaven until his enemies are his footstool, then, the church must rise to heaven. He embraced what is called 'real presence,' distinguishing it from 'physical presence.'

In Calvin's own words, "What we have so far said of the Sacrament abundantly shows that…it was ordained to be frequently used among all Christians in order that they might frequently return in memory to Christ's Passion, by such remembrance to sustain and strengthen their faith, and urge themselves to sing thanksgiving to God and to proclaim his goodness…. [T]he Lord's Table should have been spread at least once a week for the assembly of Christians, and the promises declared in it should feed us spiritually…. All, like hungry men, should flock to such a bounteous repast."[18]

In this statement, the Reformed view proposes two concurrent events in the Lord's Table. We are remembering Christ's passion and we are feeding spiritually. Although the 'real presence' position is not stated here, it is implied by seeing the Table as a place where hungry Christians come to be spiritually fed. Memorialism would say any spiritual nourishment occurring is because of our remembering the cross of Christ, and not from any active and present ministry brought about by receiving the Supper.

---

[18] John Calvin *Institutes of the Christian Religion* John T. McNeill, Editor, Ford Lewis Battles trans Library of Christian Classics (Philadelphia: Westminster, 1960 [1559]) IV.xvii.44, 46

If Memorialism is correct then why do we partake of the bread and wine? Why not just have a solemn service where we 'remember' the cross. Or better yet, why not show clips from a movie?

"In this manner, Calvin overcomes the Zwinglian problem, and demonstrates why partaking of the Supper is vital to receiving its benefits. He also shows a richer understanding of the benefits that flow from the Supper. We do not simply remember Christ's death as we partake, rather we actively feed on the body and blood of the crucified Savior."[19]

I see the Reformed view of communion as a step in the right direction from that held by Rome, and the positions of Martin Luther and Ulrich Zwingli. I believe they contributed to its recovery back to a biblical foundation. Yet, we must not stop here. We must consider the Lord's Table in light of the 'new covenant and 'kingdom eschatology.' Until these are examined we will fail to restore the Lord's Table to its proper place.

Does one of these five position reflect your view? If not, then we agree. Although there are aspects within these views which are biblical, overall, none meet the new covenant standard. Before moving on and examining Scripture for fresh insight into communion, there is one more view which needs sharing. It is called 'spiritual communion.'

A Non-Traditional View

Spiritual Communion

After reviewing the five traditional views of the Lord's Table there is one non-traditional view we should review. I call it non-traditional because I am not aware of any Christian denomination practicing it. As it is a minority position few are aware of it. It

---

[19] Matthew W. Mason, A Spiritual Banquet: John Calvin on the Lord's Supper, www.theologian.org.uk

does present several positive additions to understanding how the New Testament presents communion.

As a young man, I was presented with a view far different from my Evangelical upbringing. The best name for this view is 'spiritual communion.' Several men of God who impacted my life held this view; men like Tilford Hansen, Ray Kirschke, Evert Roberts and others. I cannot give a detailed theological apologetic for this view as none was given to me, but several major points make this unique view worth exploring. First 'spiritual communion' is as the name indicates; there is no actual receiving of the physical bread and wine. True communion is spiritual. This view sees eating small pieces of bread and drinking grape juice as a false substitute for the real thing. Those advocating this view were men who moved in the Holy Spirit and preached a present reality of the Kingdom. They were in many ways men who understood spiritual realities before their time. What they proclaimed about God's kingdom and the coming of Jesus is now taught by many. How did a revelation of the kingdom result in changing the standard view of communion? I can only speculate, but here are some thoughts.

First, they held to a basic structure of preterism (but I never heard the term from them) and may have taken I Corinthians 11:26 as meaning once Jesus returned in the first century, the taking of the 'Lord's Table' was no longer necessary. Second, and what may be the most important, is the understanding of how valuable true Christian fellowship is. I am not aware of any other teaching which presents communion in this light. As a practical matter, I have enjoyed and experienced this level of fellowship and it is truly enriching and rewarding. It brings us closer to a real sharing in the body of Christ than the majority of traditional communion services.

I Corinthians 10:1-5

For I do not want you to be unaware, brothers, that our fathers were all under the cloud, and all passed through the sea, [2] and all were baptized into Moses in the cloud and in the sea, [3] and all ate the same spiritual food, [4] and all drank the same spiritual drink. For they drank from the spiritual Rock that followed them, and the Rock was Christ. [5] Nevertheless, with most of them God was not pleased, for they were overthrown in the wilderness.

Eating and drinking under the new covenant takes us to a higher realm than the physical elements. Spiritual communion sees our fellowship with each other as a sharing of the Rock, which is Christ.

I Corinthians 10:16-17

The cup of blessing that we bless, is it not a participation in the blood of Christ? The bread that we break, is it not a participation in the body of Christ? Because there is one bread, we who are many are one body, for we all partake of the one bread.

The question is, "Can we partake in the 'body of Christ' without physically receiving bread and wine?

I Corinthians 11:23-26

For I received from the Lord what I also delivered to you, that the Lord Jesus on the night when he was betrayed took bread, and when he had given thanks, he broke it, and said, "This is my body which I s for you. Do this in remembrance of me." In the same way also he took the cup, after supper, saying, "This cup is the new covenant in my blood. Do this, as often as you drink it, in remembrance of me." For as often as you eat this bread and drink the cup, you proclaim the Lord's death until he comes.

As I began to evaluate 'spiritual communion' this verse was not part of the argument-maybe it should have been. The main reason for the non-participation was because of their understanding that Christian fellowship and sharing the word of God together is the "real" communion which doesn't depend on symbols. The day of symbols is gone and eternal realities are now our standard. As I heard many years ago, "What spiritual value can there be in a "piece of bread and sip of grape juice." The overlaying 'religious' nature of the common communion service was far removed from the revelation of a present heaven and glorious partaking of God's kingdom.

Those who embraced 'spiritual communion' felt partaking of physical elements was a step down from the realities of the kingdom. Spiritual communion restored a renewed appreciation for the deep level of fellowship available by sharing in the 'body of Christ.' For the time it was a true breakthrough from the 'unspiritual' nature of most communion services which reflected a funeral service for the dead and not a celebration of the living. If my choice was between the typical communion service I've experienced and 'spiritual communion,' I would not hesitate to embrace 'spiritual communion.' Yet, I believe we must go further. Biblical revelation increases, in each generation. From all the views presented there are good points which can be carried forward. Spiritual communion must not be forgotten and it can, as will be presented, be a foundation for a true kingdom service celebrating the presence of King Jesus.

It is easy to find fault with other theological traditions we have no experience with but a better way is to see what we can retain from each view. What in the six different views can we embrace part of the foundation for a kingdom/new covenant understanding of communion?

Transubstantiation

From the Roman Catholic position, I take one very positive element; they hold the Lord's Table in high view and make it part of their weekly worship service. If Evangelicals would make no other change than this, we will begin to recapture the essence of New Testament Christianity.

Eastern Orthodox

What may look on the outside as a very formal and institutional tradition has a solid biblical foundation which we can learn from. They focus in on the victory of Christ, with him seated in the heavens far above principalities and powers. They accept all of God's family to be partakers of the bread and wine, including children. And last, an intriguing aspect of their theology is that the 'truth' of the bread and wine can only be given by the Holy Spirit.

Consubstantiation

From the Lutheran tradition, we gain one strong element; faith. Since the whole of our Christian life begins and continues with faith and since "And without faith it is impossible to please him" (Heb. 11:6) it is a vital part of how we come to the Table of the Lord.

Memorialism

For most Evangelicals, the view they practice comes from Ulrich Zwingli. What can be gained and retained from this position? Since this was my experience growing up in a fundamentalist church, it is more difficult to find the positive from those traditions I have had little contact with. What can be said? At least in my memory the people seemed to take it seriously, and that is a good thing. The Table of the Lord is not a place to be overly causal in our attitude or flippant in our approach. With that said, the purpose of my writing is this, Memorialism is a serious departure from the New Testament revelation and the early churches experience. I find little to support it.

Reformed

Most Evangelicals and especially those in the Pentecostal/ Charismatic churches have a pejorative attitude towards the Reformed tradition and especially John Calvin, its theological founder. That debate is for another forum, yet, when it comes to the Lord's Table, I identify with the Reformed view more than the previous ones. Why? This position teaches the 'real presence' of Jesus in the communion without teaching 'physical presence.' It is not just remembering, there is a genuine presence of Christ to the believer in partaking of the elements. I like that.

Spiritual Communion

Spiritual Communion is relatively unknown, yet, if given only two choices, the traditional view of Memorialism or spiritual communion, I would opt for the latter. It is the weakness and overly religiously approach of the Evangelical view which helped lead to the conviction that true communion is a genuine and true experience with other members of the body of Christ. Holy Communion is experienced by believers as they share the life of God. Spiritual communion sees the rich fellowship of the saints as a partaking of the body of Christ. From this position, we can retain the 'spiritual aspect' of the Lord's Table and from it build a kingdom/new covenant view.

Even though these views of the Lords Table are endorsed by multitudes of Christians, I find myself looking in from the outside. Over many years, I have participated in receiving communion in churches with different views, yet my primary experience is within Evangelical Churches which practices Memorialism and perhaps this is the reason for my frustration.

Therefore, over the next chapters we will build from Scripture an alternative view. I am not doing so to be contrarian or inventive for its own sake. I believe in the church. And communion properly placed with our other doctrinal commitments will strengthen the church. I am quite appalled by how causal and non-observant many Evangelicals (especially charismatics) are toward communion. Yet, I also see how the 'modern Evangelical communion service' has little to offer, especially to those who have a kingdom/new covenant mindset. Something is missing. Things must change.

Chapter 3

The Passover

The New Testament communion celebration is derived from the Jewish Passover observance. It is in this setting that Jesus institutes the ordinance we call the Lord's Supper. In early spring the Jews of the first century kept the Passover (Pesach). This feast was kept by Jesus and recorded in two of the Gospels (Mark 14:12-26; also in Luke 2:41-43).

Mark 14:12-16

And on the first day of Unleavened Bread, when they sacrificed the Passover lamb, his disciples said to him, "Where will you have us go and prepare for you to eat the Passover?" [13] *And he sent two of his disciples and said to them, "Go into the city, and a man carrying a jar of water will meet you. Follow him,* [14] *and wherever he enters, say to the master of the house, 'The Teacher says, where is my guest room, where I may eat the Passover with my disciples?'* [15] *And he will show you a large upper room furnished and ready; there prepare for us."* [16] *And the disciples set out and went to the city and found it just as he had told them, and they prepared the Passover.*

Jesus made prior arrangements to observe the Passover with his disciples. As the two disciples went out they found everything prepared. What these followers of Jesus did not know was the significant changes about to take place.

Mark 14:22-26

And as they were eating, he took bread, and after blessing it broke it and gave it to them, and said, "Take; this is my body." [23] *And he took a cup, and when he had given thanks he gave it to them, and they all drank of it. [24] And he said to them, "This is my blood of the covenant, which is poured out for many. [25] Truly, I say to you, I will not drink again of the fruit of the vine until that day when I drink it new in the kingdom of God. [26] And when they had sung a hymn, they went out to the Mount of Olives.*

The Passover was to remember Israel's historic deliverance out of Egypt. We read this in Exodus.

Exodus 12:11-13

In this manner, you shall eat it: with your belt fastened, your sandals on your feet, and your staff in your hand. And you shall eat it in haste. It is the LORD's Passover. [12] For I will pass through the land of Egypt that night, and I will strike all the firstborn in the land of Egypt, both man and beast; and on all the gods of Egypt I will execute judgments: I am the LORD. [13] The blood shall be a sign for you, on the houses where you are. And when I see the blood, I will pass over you, and no plague will befall you to destroy you, when I strike the land of Egypt.

Jews for generations kept the Passover. They remembered how God delivered them by the power of the blood. The first Passover was significant in Israel becoming a covenant people. They were protected from judgment. "This night was to be different from all other nights. God Himself would 'pass over' and redeem every household from judgment over which was covered by the blood of the lamb. This was not an atonement sacrifice. The Israelites had not sinned. This was pure deliverance from circumstance. The yoke of Egypt and slavery was about to be thrown off and the demonic gods of Egypt judged."[20]

The Passover meal included a roasted lamb and unleavened bread (Ex. 12:8). It is interesting that "The lamb was dropped from the Seder when the temple was destroyed in A.D. 70. The use of a roasted lamb or shank-bone of lamb came back in but cooked in a

---

[20] *Jonathan Went,* PASSOVER, LAST SUPPER AND EUCHARIST, www.leaderu.com

different way to distinguish it from the Passover lamb itself."[21]
The Jews may have stopped eating the Passover lamb because they
no longer had a temple and because Jerusalem was in ruins, but as
Christians we know Jesus was the final sacrifice. The feast was
not to include foreigners unless they were circumcised (Ex.12:43,
45). Under the new covenant those in Christ are marked by a
spiritual circumcision of heart (Rom. 2:28-29) and participate in
the real Passover.

What was the 'Passover meal' like when Jesus gathered his
disciples around the table? If we study the modern celebration of
the Jewish Seder we must realize a lot has been added to the
original Old Testament practice. These oral and written traditions
are seen in both the Mishnah and the Talmud. So, we are not
exactly sure which elements were kept when Jesus and his
followers celebrated the Passover. The important aspect for us is
how Jesus used this occasion to institute a new Passover under a
different covenant, 'The Lord's Table.'

Samuele Bacchiocchi[22], former professor at Andrews University
provides background information. "Though John does not
explicitly designate the Last Supper as a Passover meal for the
reasons just mentioned, there are indications that he also regarded
the meal shared by Christ with His disciples as a paschal meal. The
meal takes place within Jerusalem even though the city was
thronged with pilgrims (John 12:12, 18, 20; 13:2; 18:1; cf. Mark
14:17). During His last stay in Jerusalem, Jesus regularly left the
holy city in the evening and went to Bethany (Mark 11:11, 19;
Luke 19:29; 21:37), but at the time of the Last Supper, He
remained in the overcrowded city. Why? Because, as mentioned
earlier, it was a rule that the paschal lamb had to be eaten within
the gates of Jerusalem. The supper is held in the evening and lasts
into the night (John 13:30; cf. Mark 14:17). The ordinary supper

---

[21] Ibid.
[22] Samuele Bacchiocchi was a Seventh-Day Adventist scholar and many of his positions I
firmly disagree with. Yet, he is recognized for his work into New Testament history and the
early church.

was not held at night, but in the late afternoon. The Last Supper began in the evening and lasted into the night because, as Joachim Jeremias explains, "the Passover had to be eaten at night ever since its institution."[23]

If you disapprove of wine drinking your involvement in this Jewish tradition is limited. We have Christians which forbid even a taste of wine at communion, so following the Jewish custom of Seder, would be extremely problematic as they were served not one but four cups of wine. Each cup of wine represented four aspects of their deliverance (Exodus 6). I remember once as a young man attending a Christian service where this tradition was kept, including multiple cups of wine. It was a service to remember, but we are not to celebrate the Lord's Table by following Jewish traditions, but by principles found in the new covenant.

In Exodus, we have the story of the first Passover. Jewish tradition grew over the years as to how they should observe the deliverance of Israel out of Egypt. Eventually, the custom of the four cups became an essential aspect of the Passover observance.

Exodus 6:6-7

Say therefore to the people of Israel, 'I am the LORD, and I will bring you out from under the burdens of the Egyptians, and I will deliver you from slavery to them, and I will redeem you with an outstretched arm and with great acts of judgment. [7] I will take you to be my people, and I will be your God, and you shall know that I am the LORD your God, who has brought you out from under the burdens of the Egyptians.

The four cups in Jewish tradition represented aspects of the original Passover.

   1. Cup one pointed to their deliverance, "I will bring you out."

---

[23] Samuele Bacchiocchi, PASSOVER IN THE NEW TESTAMENT, www.biblicalperspectives.com

2. Cup two was to remember the words "I will deliver you from slavery."
3. Cup three, "I will redeem you,"
4. Cup four "I will take you to be my people."

According to the Mishnah even the poor were to have four cups of wine to drink. When thinking about this Jewish tradition and comparing it to the actions of the Corinthian church, something was very wrong. In Corinth, it went from sharing with the poor to excluding them. This was their sin, bringing division into the church by their selfish actions.

Jewish Rabbi Naftali Silberberg comments on the use of four cups of wine.

"Wine is considered a royal drink, one that symbolizes freedom. It is the appropriate beverage for the nights when we celebrate our freedom from Egyptian bondage. Many reasons are given for drinking *four* cups of wine. Here are some of them: When promising to deliver the Jews from Egyptian slavery, G-d used four terms to describe the redemption (Exodus 6:6-8): a) "I shall *take* you out..." b) "I shall *rescue* you..." c) "I shall *redeem* you..." d) "I shall *bring* you..." The four cups symbolize our freedom from our four exiles. We were liberated from Pharaoh's four evil decrees: a) Slavery. b) The ordered murder of all male progeny by the Hebrew midwives. c) The drowning of all Hebrew boys in the Nile by Egyptian thugs. d) The decree ordering the Israelites to collect their own straw for use in their brick production. The four cups symbolize our freedom from our four exiles: The Egyptian, Babylonian, and Greek exiles, and our current exile which we hope to be rid of very soon with the coming of Moshiach."[24]

---

[24] Naftali Silberberg , Why Four Cups of Wine at the Seder, www.chabad.org (The content on this page is provided by AskMoses.com, and is copyrighted by the author, publisher, and/or AskMoses.com. You are welcome to distribute it further, provided you do not revise any part of it and you include this statement, credit the author and/or publisher, and include a link to www.AskMoses.com.)

There is an additional comment about the coming of Moshiach. (lit. "the anointed one") the Messiah. One of the 13 principles of the Jewish faith is that G-d will send the Messiah to return the Jews to the land of Israel, rebuild the <u>Holy Temple</u> and usher in the utopian Messianic Era. (lit. "the anointed one") the Messiah. One of the 13 principles of the Jewish faith is that G-d will send the Messiah to return the Jews to the land of Israel, rebuild the <u>Holy Temple</u> and usher in the utopian Messianic Era. "The anointed one" the Messiah. One of the 13 principles of the Jewish faith is that G-d will send the Messiah to return the Jews to the land of Israel, rebuild the Holy Temple and usher in the utopian Messianic era."[25]

Repeated 3X

What I find remarkable in this statement is its similarity to dispensational eschatology. Both dispensationalists and orthodox Jews teach the Messiah will return to a re-gathered Israel, worship in a new temple and then, live in the Messianic age. I disagree with premillennial eschatology. My understanding is that the age of the Kingdom began with the first coming of Jesus. By his death and resurrection, he made both Jews and Gentiles into "one new man (Eph.2:14-16). God has one people under a new covenant. God now has a temple, which is the church. The kingdom began like a mustard seed (Mt. 13: 31-32), like a small stone (Dan. 2: 35), like a growing river (Ez. 47:1-12) and like unleavened bread (Mt.13:33). There is no artificial division between the age of the church and the age of the Messianic Kingdom. With this firmly in mind our coming around the Lord's Table will have greater meaning. While Jews still wait for their Messiah, we rejoice in his finished work. We now can feast at his table.

We are not sure how closely Jesus followed the Passover traditions of his day. We do not read of the 'four cups' of wine. Following Luke's story, we know Jesus at least shared 'two cups' with his disciples. The emphasis of Luke is how Jesus abruptly changed the tradition and set forth an example for new covenant people to follow. When he took the cup after the meal he altered the

---

[25] Ibid.

program, "And he took a cup, and when he had given thanks he gave it to them, and they all drank of it. [24] And he said to them, "This is my blood of the covenant (I Cor.11:23)." Which cup was this? Was it the first of four? "It is most likely that the last supper 'cup' of wine is to be associated with **the third Passover cup, that of redemption** (Exodus 6.6), associated with the coming of Elijah and eschatological expectation of the Messiah."[26]

David Brickner on the third cup, "The New Testament names one of the cups—the cup taken after supper, which is traditionally the third cup. Jesus calls this cup "the new covenant in my blood, which is shed for you" (Luke 22:20). The Apostle Paul calls it, "the cup of blessing which we bless," as well as "the cup of the Lord" (1 Corinthians 10:16, 21)."[27]

When Jesus took the cup after the meal it was traditionally the third cup. It is this cup which becomes the sign of the new covenant. Brickner continues, "Both Jesus and Paul draw on something from Jewish tradition to provide insights not previously understood. By calling the cup "the new covenant in my blood," Jesus makes a direct reference to the promise of Jeremiah 31. God had declared that He would make a new covenant, because the previous covenant had become "broken" (Jeremiah 31:32)."[28]

We must not be dogmatic where Scripture is silent, but let's not ignore history or culture either. Both Jesus and his disciples were raised with the Jewish customs of their times and knew them well. It is reasonable to assume the cup Jesus drank with his disciples after their supper was the third cup. This is the cup of the new covenant. This leads us to the fourth cup which is never offered his disciples. We take up the mystery of the fourth cup in a latter chapter.

---

[26] *Jonathan Went,* PASSOVER, LAST SUPPER AND EUCHARIST, www.leaderu.com
[27] David Brickner, The Mystery of the Passover Cup, WWW.jewsforjesus.org
[28] Ibid.

Chapter 4

The Problem in Corinth

What was going on in Corinth? Apostle Paul writes the church to correct certain problems plaguing them. What was their greatest sin? Were they spending too much time 'speaking in tongues?' Were wrong people giving 'prophetic utterances?' The problems in Corinth were many but their principal failure was just one; division in the church. Their disunity was the core problem and primary reason for their dysfunction. How they regarded the Lord's Table was a sign of this division.

Paul in his first letter to the believers in Corinth addresses the problem of division.

But I, brothers, could not address you as spiritual people, but as people of the flesh, as infants in Christ. [2] I fed you with milk, not solid food, for you were not ready for it. And even now you are not yet ready, [3] for you are still of the flesh. For while there is jealousy and strife among you, are you not of the flesh and behaving only in a human way? [4] For when one says, "I follow Paul," and another, "I follow Apollos," are you not being merely human (I Cor. 3:1-4)?

Apostle Paul wished the church was maturing in the faith and ready for spiritual 'solid food.' But they were still 'infants in Christ.' There is nothing fundamentally wrong being an infant if you were recently born. An adult person acting like a baby is another matter. By this time, Paul figured enough time has passed for them to grow up in their faith, but he was wrong. The signs of their immaturity were their "jealousy and strife."

Jealousy and strife can disguise themselves in 'super-spiritual' clothing. Some Corinthian Christians may have boasted that they were 'personally trained by Apostle Paul.' Others were equally prideful of their spiritual father, Apollos. These situations are found in modern churches. It brings division and causes the church to function and be seen as a 'merely human' institution. Paul's message was straightforward; grow up.

As we follow Paul's letter it gets even more serious.

Do you not know that you are God's temple and that God's Spirit dwells in you? [17] *If anyone destroys God's temple, God will destroy him. For God's temple is holy, and you are that temple (1 Cor.3:16-17).*

This verse is often used God's warning against committing suicide. As serious as suicide is, I do not think Apostle Paul had this in mind. He was addressing the church and the serious consequences of division. For those, because of their willful and unrepentant "jealously and strife", were in actuality working to destroy the temple of God; which is the church. He was addressing a corporate problem.

With this as our background we can better understand the serious nature of how the Corinthians observed the Lord's Table. They were a divided and carnal church.

But in the following instructions I do not commend you, because when you come together is not for the better but for the worse (1 Cor. 11:17)

This is a sad commentary for the local church Paul founded. They would have been better off canceling their church service. They were making things worse when they gathered for worship. How can that be? Their division gave way to extreme selfishness in their observance of the 'love feast' and celebrating the Lord's Table. At this junction, a brief history on the love feast is in order. The Christians in Corinth were not hording the mini glasses of wine and small amounts of bread. The love feast was a full meal and those who brought no provision were not invited to share, they were left out.

The Love Feast

The love feast was a full meal and part of normal first century apostolic worship. This 'love feast' was also called the agape by early Christians. This custom remained in the Christian church longer than most think. "Even after the death of the apostles, the pre-Nicene Church continued to practice the agape or love feast. Yet, within a century or so after Constantine's conversion, this important part of apostolic worship totally disappeared."[29] In our passage from Paul he reminds us Jesus used the shared meal to introduce what we know as communion. "In the same way also he took the cup, after supper (1 Cor. 11:25)." So, in this context of a meal taken together the institution of communion was born.

When Luke writes the history of the first church he provides the main reasons why they these believers gathered.

And they devoted themselves to the apostles' teaching and the fellowship, to the breaking of bread and the prayers. [43] And awe came upon every soul, and many wonders and signs were being done through the apostles. [44] And all who believed were together and had all things in common. [45] And they were selling their possessions and belongings and distributing the proceeds to all, as any had need. [46] And day by day, attending the temple together and breaking bread in their homes, they received their food with glad and generous hearts (Acts 2:42-46).

The 'breaking of bread' certainly refers to their regular receiving of the Lord's Table. Yet, they also shared meals, they were "breaking bread in their homes, they received their food with glad and generous hearts." The early church was marked by generous hearts and joy as they came together.

---

[29] Scroll Publishing Co, www.scrollpublishng.com

From the Evangelical Dictionary of Theology; "Certainly by the time of Paul's writing to the Corinthians (ca. AD 55) it is evident that that church observed the practice of meeting together for a common meal before partaking of the Lord's Supper (1 Cor. 11:17-34). ...The situation described here is possible only in the context of a meal more substantial than, and preceding the bread and wine of the Lord's Supper."[30]

In 1 Corinthians 11 Paul makes it clear they were gathering not just to receive the elements of the Lord's Table (wine and bread), they were having a meal, and this is where the problems began. "For in eating, each one goes ahead with his own meal (vs. 21). This was supposed to be a 'love feast' and a time of sharing God's goodness with one another. Instead the Corinthians turned it into a selfish time of excluding the poor who had nothing to bring. I have never seen anyone drinking to the extent of drunkenness during communion. The amount of wine given is far insufficient. This was during the time of the 'love feast.' What we call 'communion' came at the end of meal.

In the book of Jude there is a reference to the love feast.

These are hidden reefs at your love feasts, as they feast with you without fear, shepherds feeding themselves; waterless clouds, swept along by winds; fruitless trees in late autumn, twice dead, uprooted; [13] wild waves of the sea, casting up the foam of their own shame; wandering stars, for whom the gloom of utter darkness has been reserved forever (Jude 12-13).

Unbelievers during this period of the church were mingling with believers. These were not 'seekers' considering the claims of Jesus. Jude says they are of such evil that 'utter darkness' awaits their future. What we learn here, despite the emphasis upon these 'wandering stars', is thirty years after Pentecost, the church remained committed to the 'love feast.'

---

[30] Evangelical Dictionary of Theology, Walter A. Elwell (Editor), Baker Academic; 2 edition (May 1, 2001), p.660

Since it is clear the 'love feast' followed by the 'Lord's Supper' was normal in the early church, why did it eventually stop? Slowly, maybe because of abuses or of the practicality the meal (love feast), the Lord's Supper and agape feast were separated. According to notes from the *Geneva Bible of 1599* it was the Apostle Paul who stopped the love feast. "The Apostle thinketh it good to take away the love feasts, for their abuse, although they had been a long time, and with commendation used in Churches, and were appointed and instituted by the Apostles.[31] I see no where that Paul forbid having a common meal (love feast) but rather their abuse of it. And we know from history it was the rule of the church for a number of years. "Nevertheless, even though the agape and communion went their separate ways, the church continued to practice both of them until sometime after the time of Constantine."[32]

We must remember, Sunday in the early church was a work day, so they met very early for worship. As time went on, some churches met for the Lord's Supper in the morning and then, gathered in the evening for the 'love feast.' According to The Encyclopedia of Early Christianity, "Eventually, abuses, coupled with imperial rescripts forbidding the meals of secret societies, brought about the separation of the fraternal meal (agape) and Eucharist, but not everywhere and not at once. In Ignatius (ca. 110), for instance, the celebration of the agape is related to but distinct from the Eucharist; so also, the Didache. In Justin Martyr, the Eucharist seems to have absorbed the fraternal functions characteristic of agape. ...On the other hand, in Clement's Alexandria (ca. 200) agape and Eucharist are joined, in spite of the signal abuses to which Clement gives witness."[33]

---

[31] *1599 Geneva Bible* (White Hall, WV: Telle Lege Press, 2006), p. 1180.
[32] Steve Atkerson, The Lord's Supper-A Holy Meal, http://www.ntrf.org
[33] The Encyclopedia of Early Christianity, Routledge, 2 Sub edition, 1997

As time progressed eventually all the churches from different regions separated the meal from the Lord's Table and then the meal became less often and in most cases dropped all together.

Should we in our quest for authentic New Testament practice restore the 'love feast?' Should leaders only serve the Lord's Table when a full meal can be arranged for the church? For practical reasons, it may not be workable. Many local churches do not have facilities for such activities. Churches with less than 150-200 members at times can accommodate their congregations for a meal, but once a church grows larger it becomes difficult. Yet, if the church is not gathering to eat it is missing a key element in advancing relationships in the church. Greeting one another for a few seconds once a week will not build strong family unity in a local church. Because of this, churches have started home groups so this type of fellowship can continue. The specialness of eating together cannot be undervalued. It is essential for local churches to find a way in which the congregation can share meals together.

As for being obedient to Scripture, I see nothing which requires a full meal be taken before we partake of the wine and bread during the Lord's Supper. This is part of our worship service and the focus is on our Lord, proclaiming what he accomplished on the cross and celebrating the fullness of his kingdom. It does not replace times of deep 'relationship building' which comes naturally from sharing a meal, but neither does communion require it.

Paul reminds the wayward Corinthians of why they gather in the first place. *"When you come together, it is not the Lord's Supper that you eat (1 Cor.11:20)."* The primary purpose of gathering was to receive the Lord's Supper. This causes me to wonder what the Apostle Paul would say to modern churches concerning how we observe communion. He cannot scold us for improperly conducting the 'love feast.' And since many churches have communion so seldom, any practical discussion of issues many seem for him a waste of time. I'm not sure how Paul would instruct us, but I think a stirring word would be in order. I cannot see Paul nor any of the Apostles, or any New Testament Christians going months without coming to the Table of our Lord. It would have been unthinkable. The Lord's Table is one key feature which identified them as Christians.

1 Corinthians 11:21-22

For in eating, each one goes ahead with his own meal. One goes hungry, another gets drunk. [22] What! Do you not have houses to eat and drink in? Or do you despise the church of God and humiliate those who have nothing? What shall I say to you? Shall I commend you in this? No, I will not.

There are times where a father must bring discipline to his children. Here, Paul, the spiritual father of the church in Corinth, addresses a serious problem. They were gathering for their love feast and instead of sharing with the poor (as in the Passover) some were hording their food and wine for themselves. Only those able to afford to bring food were eating and drinking. A few drank so much wine they were getting drunk. Paul tells them in so many words, "If you want to get drunk and gorge yourself with food, do it at home." There was nothing wrong per say with eating or drinking, but the manner in which it was done exhibited a selflessness not acceptable for believers in Jesus. They were shaming the poor and bringing humiliation upon their brothers and sisters in the Lord. This was their sin; therefore, serious consequences resulted.

In Evangelical churches the emphasis upon searching your heart for sin is prevalent. We are warned by the pastor about receiving the communion elements if we have sin in our lives. The basis for this dire warning comes from the Apostle Paul is words in 1 Corinthians 11. It results in a time of silence where we all attempt to remember what sin we may have committed during the week, or since our last communion service.

Receiving Communion in an Unworthy Manner

1 Corinthians 11:27

Whoever, therefore, eats the bread or drinks the cup of the Lord in an unworthy manner will be guilty concerning the body and blood of the Lord.

Have you felt unworthy during the communion service? When the Pastor predicts sickness or even death it becomes rather uncomfortable. Yet, we must partake or what will those around us think? While serving the Lord's Table in Bulgaria I noticed it is common for many to pass the elements along without partaking; even among the church faithful. At least they have more concern for what God thinks than their fellow church members. Yet, is all this introspection, looking for sin, useful? Is Paul demanding this of the Corinthians?

First of all, if during the communion service the Holy Spirit reminds you of sin, then you have one simple reaction; repent. No one should have to coerce you. Then, you are fully prepared to receive communion. Is it actual sin which is preventing Christians from partaking of the Lord's Supper? I do not think so. The problem is they FEEL sinful, they FEEL unworthy. They feel polluted by the world, they feel they have failed the Lord, their family and themselves. Add to this guilt all the words from the Pastor and it is a miracle anyone partakes.

The reason for all this 'feeling of being unworthy' is simple; bad teaching. If we were taught simple truths found in the new covenant, we would come with joy to the Table of the Lord, not trembling or afraid we are damning ourselves to hell. Has Jesus forgiven your sin? Are we made righteous in his sight or not? Communion and its meaning cannot be separated from the other great foundational truths of the Bible.

We come to the Table, not in our works or by any self-improvement, but we come in the 'righteousness of Christ.' He alone is the one who makes us worthy. If we pass the elements during communion, what are we saying about the sacrifice of Jesus on the cross? Was it enough or not?

Apostle Paul was addressing those Corinthians who were being greedy with their food and wine, shaming the poor and bringing division into the church. It was their actions he was speaking against. It was their "unworthy manner" in terms of how they conducted themselves. This was their sin.

Hebrews 10:9-14

Then he added, "Behold, I have come to do your will." He does away with the first in order to establish the second. ¹⁰ And by that will we have been sanctified through the offering of the body of Jesus Christ once for all. And every priest stands daily at his service, offering repeatedly the same sacrifices, which can never take away sins. ¹² But when Christ had offered for all time a single sacrifice for sins, he sat down at the right hand of God, ¹³ waiting from that time until his enemies should be made a footstool for his feet. ¹⁴ For by a single offering he has perfected for all time those who are being sanctified.

In the book of Hebrews, we find good news for everyone walking in Christ. The author explains how the Messiah does away "with the first" to "establish the second." What is first? It is the requirements of the law; the old covenant. What is the second? The second is the "offering of the body of Jesus Christ." Then comes the good news. The author states that by this offering of Jesus "we have been sanctified." After the cross and resurrection Jesus ascends to heaven where he now reigns over his kingdom. The 'right hand of God' is the place of authority. In the book of Hebrews, we have words which should set us free from guilt, condemnation, and all other attempts to arrive at perfection. *"For by a single offering he has perfected for all time those who are being sanctified (Heb.10:14)."* There is a life time process of renewing our minds and walking in what we have been given, yet, it is clear, by the cross of Jesus, "he has perfected us for all time."

When we come to the Table of the Lord, we do so as those who are perfected not as someone striving to attain perfection. When we accept, we are righteous because of the sacrifice of Christ, we will no longer judge ourselves or others as being worthy or unworthy of receiving communion. For those battling with temptation, there is a place at the table for you. Come in faith, not in your own works or ability to overcome sin, but come with the knowledge you have been cleansed, you have been made righteous. No one has a greater right to receive communion than you do!

Ephesians 4:23-24

And to be renewed in the spirit of your minds, and to put on the new self, created after the likeness of God in true righteousness and holiness.

When a person comes to Christ, they receive a new nature. Apostle Paul says we put on a 'new self.' What is the nature of this 'new person' we have become? First, we have not disappeared, we have been redeemed. 'In Christ' we are the true person we were created to be. The utter failure of Christians attempting to put to death 'self' is an endless process. The fact is, we are a "new self", it is made in 'true righteousness.' We are pure, holy, and totally acceptable in the sight of God...right now!

When you come to the Table of the Lord feeling down, like a failure, like you have been run over with a truck, then, take the opportunity to receive grace and strength from the communion. It is what you need! The communion is provided to nourish you not to judge you! Come rejoicing in the finished work of Jesus on your behalf. Your sins are forgiven, you are a child of God. You are in Christ. You are a member of the Christian community. Drink the wine, eat the bread, and celebrate the wonder and awe of the new covenant.

Discerning the Body of the Lord

We are not partaking communion by refusing to share our food or wine, so we are good, right? Then the Pastor reads on and it gets worse.

For anyone who eats and drinks without discerning the body eats and drinks judgment on himself. That is why many of you are weak and ill, and some have died (1 Cor. 11:29-30).

What does it mean to 'discern the body?' We cannot overlook that Paul had in mind the physical body of Jesus on the cross. Yet, because of his prior statement, we must go beyond this obvious statement.

Because there is one bread, we who are many are one body, for we all partake of the one bread (1 Cor. 10:17).

I like The Message version of this passage.

1 Corinthians 10:15-18

I assume I'm addressing believers now who are mature. Draw your own conclusions: When we drink the cup of blessing, aren't we taking into ourselves the blood, the very life, of Christ? And isn't it the same with the loaf of bread we break and eat? Don't we take into ourselves the body, the very life, of Christ? Because there is one loaf, our many-ness becomes one-ness—Christ doesn't become fragmented in us. Rather, we become unified in him. We don't reduce Christ to what we are; he raises us to what he is. That's basically what happened even in old Israel—those who ate the sacrifices offered on God's altar entered into God's action at the altar.

As discussed previously, there are numerous biblical scholar who say the 'cup of blessing' is the third cup in the Passover celebration. It is this cup which Jesus essentially says, 'This cup is the new covenant.' It is a cup of blessing not a cup of judgment. From it we are enriched by the very life of Christ.

How do we discern the body? What body is Paul speaking of? Should we discern our own physical body? Or does Paul refer to the one 'body of Christ,' the church? Because Paul talks about the 'one bread, I believe the best interpretation is that we are all part of the 'body' of Jesus. We are the body of Christ. If we wrongly discern the 'body' it is because we are not viewing the church correctly. We are allowing division to enter our relationships. We are allowing greed and pride free access in the church.

When we receive communion, it testifies to our unity, to our oneness in Christ, therefore, division in the church results in judgment upon us. Should there be a time for reflection before coming to the Table? Yes, yet, do not get wrapped up in your personal failures but allow the Holy Spirit to reveal damages in your relationships within the body. If you sense something, go, ask forgiveness, and then, partake together as fellow members of the new covenant. Pastors and leaders who teach communion in this fashion should allow time for fellowship and the mending of relationships before receiving the elements.

1 Corinthians 11:33-34

So then, my brothers, when you come together to eat, wait for one another—if anyone is hungry, let him eat at home—so that when you come together it will not be for judgment. About the other things I will give directions when I come.

Paul's final words about 'right conduct' for the love feast and communion shows how caring for one another is the important aspect of coming together. If you are so hungry you become a 'selfish pig' during the potluck, eat first at home. We are to honor one another by waiting for all to arrive. In this fashion, with concern for decency and love for each other, we will avoid judging ourselves by our self-inflected divisions.

Even though a few Christians have the revelation of taking the communion by themselves at home, here, Paul is stressing the community aspect of eating at the Table of the Lord. The main concept is that we are to come together as the church and receive together. Coming into true communion with other believers is more difficult than receiving it ourselves, yet, it is where the blessing lies. Unity in the church, not separating from it, is the aim of Paul.

What were the problems in Corinth?

1. They were being greedy and selfish.
2. They were shaming the poor.
3. They were failing to 'discern the body' of the Lord.

Jon Zens, a theologian and advocate of New Covenant Theology, makes a persuasive statement about the early church.

"In the New Testament we should be struck by the utter *simplicity* that characterized life in the early churches... As time elapsed, the visible church lost its original simplicity and became enmeshed in a quagmire of ecclesiastical machinery and theological speculation. The Lord's Supper is a case in point."[34]

I agree, the church became "a quagmire of ecclesiastical machinery." Communion did not escape this evolution of making complicated the simple. Centuries later we are left to unravel the mess. We have either ignored it because it seems to suppress our spontaneous and free worship, or we have created artificial rules. As a Bible student (years ago) a controversy broke about because a few students took communion by themselves in a prayer meeting. The problem was resolved without officials taking a stand on the subject. Can a group of believers take communion even without a Pastor or Elder present? This begs the question; can any believer serve the Lord's Table? Or, is it best to restrict the officiating to

---

[34] Jon Zens, The Lord's Supper, hptt://www.auburn.edu

ordained clergy.   Does the New Testament address any of these issues?

Even though most churches only have ordained clergy serve the Lord's Table, it is from tradition and not an explicit word in Scripture. Paul, nor any other New Testament author places restrictions on serving communion. Common sense should prevail. We want mature believers who understand and appreciate what they are serving. It is always good for whoever is leading to review the basic teaching of the Table. Therefore, the Elders of the church are the most suited for this task.   Yet, we must refrain from legalists rules. If a home group wants to share in the Lord's Table and there is no Elder present, I see no reason for restrictions.   We are celebrating the new covenant because of the sacrifice of Jesus. We are celebrating our unity as Christians.   As Paul said, *"let all things be done decently and in order* (1 Cor. 14:40).*"*

Modern Corinth

As we study the failures of the Corinthians we may feel a bit smug because we have no such problems. Yet, we have created problems of our own. We are not hording our food, but we have added unbiblical traditions and foolish beliefs to our celebration of communion.

Passing the Elements

One of our deep failures is a lack of teaching concerning communion.   Leaders read the Scriptures, especially about not partaking if you are unworthy, but rarely explain them.   This lack of teaching creates a void which is quickly filled with religious tradition. I have noticed over the years that there are many 'unwritten rules' which the faithful observe.   It is amazing how quickly new members pick up on these unspoken traditions and adopt them.

One of these 'rules' is, if you are not at the top of your 'spiritual life', then by all means, pass the plate. Do not receive communion if you are feeling down, forgot to pray, have neglected to read your Bible during the week, had a bad thought, or are not feeling righteous at the moment. The worst thing you can do is to eat and drink damnation upon yourself.

As seen in our conversation about the Corinthians, their private sin was not the issue, it was their public display of greed and division, which drew the rebuke from Apostle Paul. Unless you are acting out in the worst case imaginable, and by your actions dividing the church, you can and should receive communion.

Pastors have shared that the reason members regularly refuse communion is because, 'We do not know what is going on in people's lives and what kind of sin they may have committed.' This is true, we really do not know. Yet, why would any serious Christian, while waiting for the elements to come their way, having become aware of sin in their life, not repent of it immediately, and be free to partake?

The Lord's Table is not a 'high end' restaurant for the privileged. It is not the exclusive domain of staunch church members with their "I've arrived, and you have not," attitude. It is not for the 'super spiritual.' The Table of the Lord is open to all who are under his covenant. This includes children of believing parents. The Lord's Table is open for the depressed, the confused, the weak, people with physical disabilities, and those with mental and emotional problems. The communion service displays our unity not our division.

Piling on the Guilt

The bottom line for many is that 'Communion Sunday' is about measuring our guilt. We often leave with another reason to feel guilty. In many of these religiously oriented communion services, Christians who feel guilt, but take the communion anyway, do so because they want to maintain their 'high spiritual status.' "If I pass the elements without partaking, others will think I'm a great sinner." Therefore, they leave with even more guilt than when they came in.

If you have a deep sense of guilt without relief, you need communion. Of course, repent when the Spirit convicts you, but live without condemnation. Paul said it best, "There is therefore now no condemnation for those who are in Christ Jesus (Romans 8:1)." We live under a new covenant, we are forgiven, therefore, we should partake of communion with joy and thanksgiving.

Chapter 5

Blessing-Grace-Covenant

There are three aspects of the Lord's Table which show God at work in the communion experience. The first is the blessing we receive. Second, is the work of grace in our lives. The third is how partaking of communion is an act of renewing the new covenant.

The Cup of Blessing

1 Corinthians 10:16-17

*The **cup of blessing** that we bless, is it not a participation in the blood of Christ? The bread that we break, is it not a participation in the body of Christ? Because there is one bread, we who are many are one body, for we all partake of the one bread.*

What is this 'Cup of Blessings' Paul writes about?

Matthew 26:26-28

Now as they were eating, Jesus took bread, and after blessing it broke it and gave it to the disciples, and said, "Take, eat; this is my body." And he took a cup, and when he had given thanks he gave it to them, saying, "Drink of it, all of you, for this is my blood of the covenant, which is poured out for many for the forgiveness of sins.

No matter what verse we read, the concept of unity stands out. When we receive the cup, it is to be a 'cup of blessing.' When we break and eat the bread and when we drink the wine, we are participating in the life of Christ. We are in this 'life' with each other. The community of believers share Christ with each other.

When we drink the wine of communion we drink the 'cup of blessing.' If only the church would focus on the blessing of the Lord's Table instead of hovering over people's heads the threat of judgment. Our time at the Table would then be a true blessing to all. When will leadership of local churches begin to offer communion at a higher frequency? It will happen when the congregation wants it more. And when will this happen? When leaders teach it. Revelation of Scripture brings forth hunger in people.

Many years ago, I was part of a network of churches which served the Lord's Table every Sunday. We lacked teaching on its real meaning, nevertheless, it was a regular part of our Lord's Day service. I never remember anyone complaining of its frequency. It made Sunday different and special from the other services. It was when we came as families and ate from the Lord's Table. People came and knelt, received the bread and wine, then, the elders blessed the people. It was good.

Means of Grace

Receiving communion is more than a walk down memory lane, it is a 'Means of Grace.' Within large sections of the Evangelical Church and particularly in Pentecostal/Charismatic churches the concept of 'Means of Grace' is not widely known, although in traditional protestant churches it is taught. Nevertheless, a proper understanding of communion includes it being a 'Means of Grace.'

Theologian Wayne Grudem in his Systematic Theology says, "We must be careful here, as with baptism, to avoid the mistake of overreacting to Roman Catholic teaching and maintaining that the Lord's Supper is merely symbolic and not a means of grace. Paul says, *"The cup of blessing which we bless, is it not a participation* (GK. Koinōnia "sharing," "fellowship") *in the blood of Christ?* The bread which we break, is it not a participation (koinōnia) in the body of Christ?" 1 Cor. 10:16). Because there is such a sharing in the body and blood of Christ (apparently meaning a sharing in the benefits of Christ's body and blood given for us), the unity of believers is beautifully exhibited at the time of the Lord's Supper."[35]

I agree with Grudem. Evangelicals tend to over react and therefore end up with a communion theology much less than what Scripture teaches. We need grace. Grace is more than a onetime event at our salvation. God has given the church a variety of means in which grace is continually ministered, and coming to the Table of the Lord is one of them.

John Wesley

"By 'means of grace' I understand outward signs, words, or actions, ordained of God, and appointed for this end, to be the ordinary channels whereby he might convey to men, preventing, justifying, or sanctifying grace...The chief of these means are prayer, whether in secret or with the great congregation; searching the Scriptures; (which implies reading, hearing, and meditating thereon;) and receiving the Lord's Supper, eating bread and drinking wine in remembrance of Him: And these we believe to be ordained of God, as the ordinary channels of conveying his grace to the souls of men."[36]

R. Scott Clark, academic dean and assistant professor at Westminster Seminary in California, makes an amazing appraisal (especially since he is most likely a Cessationist). After telling a story from the period of the Protestant Reformation where two well-known men almost came to physical blows over the communion, he asks why modern Christians are not so devoted to the Lord's Table. He says, "Why? It is because we have become

---

[35] Wayne Grudem, Systematic Theology, Inter-Varsity Press, Leicester, England, 1994, p.954-955
[36] John Wesley, Wesley Center Online, The Sermons of John Wesley - Sermon 16,The Means of Grace, http://wesley.nnu.edu/john-wesley/the-sermons

practically anti-supernatural and simultaneously super-spiritual in our theology."[37]

Is this the foundation of our boredom and lackadaisical attitude towards communion? Have we placed the Lord's Table as a time of sad remembrance of the cross and removed the supernatural from our experience? It is time for change. For those who believe in the continuation of the gifts of the Holy Spirit, we should expect the time of communion be one of healing and manifestation of the gifts of the Holy Spirit. Let's return the supernatural to the Lord's Table. If the church views the Table of the Lord as a special time for miracles and extraordinary events, having it more often would not be a problem. When we approach the Lord's Table in this way it is certainly a means of God's grace being manifested to the church.

During the Protestant Reformation, it was generally accepted that communion was very important and a 'means of grace.' "For both Luther and Calvin, the Supper was of critical importance as a means of grace, as a testimony to Christ's finished work, and as a seal of His work for us. Furthermore, it was a means by which our union and fellowship with the risen Christ and with one another was strengthened and renewed."[38]

God is present and active when his people come to the Table of the Lord. This may seem obvious, but it is counter to the standard doctrine of communion that many were raised with; which is the Zwingli form of memorialism. In fact, we were told over and over, 'Nothing is happening here,' "We are only remembering."

No matter what we think should happen, or what our actual experience is, God is always at work in our lives when we partake of the Lord's Table.

---

[37] R. Scott Clark, The Evangelical Fall from the Means of Grace-The Lord's Supper, http://www.the-highway.com/supper_Clark.html
[38] R. Scott Clark, The Evangelical Fall from the Means of Grace-The Lord's Supper, http://www.the-highway.com/supper_Clark.html

Real Presence of Christ

A key difference in what I am calling 'Kingdom Communion' from what most Evangelical are used to-memorialism-is embracing the active presence of Christ. If there is one central theme I wish to communicate, it is centered on the 'real presence' of Jesus in the communion. As Evangelicals, we have undervalued the presence of Christ in the communion. We seem to pride ourselves that we have 'no presence' in our service. I am not advocating any type of physical presence nor do I desire communion to become so mystical we are unable to understand it. We must move beyond our standard doctrine where we deem the Lord's Table as 'mere memory.' It is time to contend for the real and spiritual presence of Jesus. This approach takes the Scripture seriously. It offers a dose of objectivity back into our worship. And it strengthens the church with true spiritual substance.

There are two opinions about how we receive this 'real presence' in communion. Those following the Swiss Reformation of Calvin believed the church joins the heavenly worship service on the Lord's Day. As John did in the fourth chapter of Revelation, so does the church. Others see the real presence as Christ departing his heavenly position and joining the church on earth during the communion. A debate on where Christ is during the communion is a little like arguing over how many angels can stand on the point of a needle. Yes, Christ is positionally in heaven at the right hand of the Father. From his throne, he rules over all creation and is head of the church. Yet, at the same time he is in the church. He is with the church.

Our attempt to place the Ascended Christ in heaven or on earth may derive from our misunderstanding of how the New Testament views the church. The believers official position is "in Christ" in the heavens. So, whether we recognize it or not, we are already in heaven. I admit, this does not bode well with my human reasoning, nevertheless, it is true. Paul makes this clear in Ephesians. *"And raised us up with him and seated us with him in the heavenly places in Christ Jesus (Eph. 2:6)*." There is a realm in which we live in heaven, yet, on the practical level most Christians are far more aware of 'earthly things' than that of 'heavenly things.' We are people of this physical earth, this is how we are created and is part of our eternal destiny.

Though our official position is in heaven, many lack awareness of it. I believe we will have seasonal breakthroughs where this awareness will increase. It may be only a moment during worship or prayer. It may happen at any moment, where our minds become awakened to our oneness with Christ in heaven. Perhaps this is an aspect of kingdom growth we can anticipate. Every time we gather for worship, especially when we partake of the Lord's Supper, we can believe for a greater awareness of this heavenly perspective. We must go beyond the standard thinking of, "We are on earth and when we die we go to heaven." This is part of *"Your kingdom come, your will be done, on earth as it is in heaven* (Matt. 6:10). We are not required to die and go to heaven to experience the presence of Christ in heaven.

We are not gathered at the communion table to focus on our sin. Scripture is clear *"Do this in remembrance of me* (1 Corinthians 11:25)." We are to remember Jesus, not ourselves.

Can you imagine being invited to a Thanksgiving dinner where you sit at the table, not do a real meal, but a table full of beautiful color pictures? One by one you pass the pictures to the next person, take in the imaginary smell and taste of each item. We would quickly abandon the Thanksgiving tradition if this was the case. Have we done the same to the Lord's Table?

Simple terms to define our theology, is inadequate. The best term which describes what is happening during communion is "Dynamic Presence." We are never without the 'real presence' of Jesus through the power of the Holy Spirit. He is always with us in a 'real' way. Therefore, using dynamic to explain the churches experience in communion is a better description.

Evangelicals reject the 'physical presence' of the Catholics, Lutherans and Orthodox. Therefore, in our distain we reacted by claiming 'no presence.' By adopting Zwingli's 'memorialism' Evangelicals removed communion from the center of worship, seeing it as a 'non-essential' part of Sunday worship. Since there is nothing 'real' about communion its importance sunk like a rock. Receiving the Lord's Table in many local churches is monthly, quarterly or on a 'whenever' bases. By assigning a lessor value to communion we have turned our services into either preaching centers or celebrative singing centers, or both. Some churches have even become entrainment centers. We need to rethink what a Christian worship service should be.

I hear the argument against regular (weekly) communion because of the 'routine' factor. "We must not allow communion to become routine by observing it too often." Yes, Christians are susceptible to going through the motions. But why is communion the only aspect of worship we treat this way? "We want communion to be special," is another argument. To these I would respond by asking several questions. "In your church, do you take the offering weekly?" If we want giving to be special, should we limit it to once a month? "How about praying? Should we avoid praying every week so it is 'special?'" "Do you preach every week?" The problem with the 'routine' argument is we use it only for communion.

Another argument against regular communion is the time factor. "I would have to cut my sermon if we had communion every Sunday." People want their 'worship' in neat packages, and by adding something new, it would disrupt the time we have for worship. This can be true, it does take time, so we must determine if it is really worth it or not.

Another possible objection goes like this, "Our church is based upon being positive and portraying a joyous attitude; communion makes people introspective and serious." This can be a problem, but the problem is not with communion but with our Evangelical tradition of communion.

What is the real reason for not serving communion on a regular basis? It is simple. Most of us do not consider it a vital part of the normal worship service! It is extra, something we add on occasionally. If churches believed communion was an important part of worship, things would change...for the better!

Covenant Renewal

Another important aspect of communion is seen from the perspective of the church. When God's people partake of the Lord's Table we experience a renewing of the covenant. There is one major aspect of this 'renewing' which needs to be highlighted. 'Covenant renewal' is a concept which speaks to our experience. The actual work of establishing the new covenant by Jesus was and is forever a onetime experience. This must be clear. There is no actual 'reenactment' of the historic events. With this clearly in mind we then move forward to why the church is benefited from seeing the Lord's Table as 'covenant renewal.'

Covenant renewal takes us from a private exercise of spirituality to the church in its corporate expression. This also involves more than just the time of communion but considers the entire worship service a renewal of the new covenant. Theologian James Jordon speaks of a time when he was a pastor with visitors from different churches. Many of the visitors whom viewed the Lord's Table as a quick fix and not part of the overall worship of the church.

"What was in these people's minds? Clearly, they thought of communion as some kind of religious drug, a "Jesus fix" where they could come to the communion rail, then go their merry way. They did not consider the worship service a corporate event, or they would have engaged the community from start to finish. They did not view communion as part of the covenant renewal, or they would have participated in the entire service. Instead, they viewed the bread and wine magically: Jesus had been dummied down into the bread and wine by the "consecration," receiving some kind of spiritual dope by eating communion. The instant you remove communion from the covenant renewal as a whole, you raise a question to its meaning which the Bible cannot answer. The Biblical answer to the meaning of communion is this the climax of the covenant renewal, the point at which the renewal is *sealed* by a common meal. If you don't have communion in your worship service, you have not had covenant renewal. By the same token, if you don't have the Word first, you have not had covenant renewal either, because there is no covenant to seal! [39]

Viewing communion in this fashion removes any tendency to see it as 'Christian magic.' When we view the entire Sunday worship service as the renewing our covenant, receiving communion is the final seal to our entire time of worship. This is lacking in many Evangelical churches. Our worship is disjointed, often chaotic, and at times heading in no particular direction. A worship service should be a flow of life with a deliberate direction. This can be accomplished without hindering the Holy Spirit. Have we fallen into the trap of thinking the Holy Spirit can only lead when it is spontaneous? Have we fallen into thinking that 'confusion' is real freedom? Let us restore the Lord's Table to our Sunday worship service, so we 'seal' our cooperate gathering. Too many depart from our Sunday service feeling like something is missing. Can it be they are hungry for the Table of the Lord?

When there is exuberant praise, deep worship, gifts of power in display, strong biblical preaching, it is only fitting we end our time together by eating from the Lord's Table. I have attended churches where at the end of every Sunday morning worship communion is taken. It brings a completion to our time together. It enhances our unity. It strengthens our love for one another. It completes our worship together.

---

[39] James Jordon, Biblical Horizons Number 30, 1993, http://www.biblicalhorizons.com

As the body of Jesus-the church-gathers at the Lord's Table there becomes the heightened awareness of the covenantal blessings we possess. In Christ, we come to communion with faith for we are gathering with the saints in heaven to participate in their worship. Even if few have this awareness or even if there is no experience to prove it, this is our posture as we receive the elements. Why is there so little of this awareness or experience of being in heaven? Because we do not believe it? Why? Because we are not taught it.

Once leaders of local congregations teaching 'kingdom communion', faith will increase and people will desire the Table more frequently. As God's people gather with faith in the 'real presence' of Jesus, our participation in a heavenly worship service, will break through with awareness and experience. When this occurs, expect healings, miracles, and the prophetic word to make a dramatic increase in our midst.

Kingdom Communion is more than the remembering of how much Jesus did for us, and being thankful for the new covenant. Remembering is good, and with most areas of life how we 'think' is directly related to what we experience and walk in. By 'covenant renewal' we go deeper, further than just remembering.

As Baptism is a sign of our beginning steps into the new covenant, receiving communion is a sign of our continuation in that precious, dynamic Covenant.

Chapter 6

Until He Comes

Contemporary communion is based on 'remembering' the death of Jesus until the time of the "Second Coming.' Is this what Paul was writing about? If not, how did he understand 'coming?' We are now confronted with eschatology and how communion and the 'end times' are connected. I want to explore a different path, one less traveled, but one that fits the comprehensive story of the New Testament.

Pastors, authors and commentaries line up in great numbers to explain Paul when he wrote, *"For as often as you eat this bread and drink the cup, you proclaim the Lord's death until he comes (1 Cor. 11;26).* The conclusion of many is *"Until he comes"* refers to the "Second Coming." It seems simple, Jesus was about to die and he knew it. There would not be another Passover observance with his disciples. Therefore, he tells them in the future he will drink it once again and we immediately conclude this means the Second Coming. I would like to explore a different conclusion.

It is not possible to turn a book on communion into a fully developed study of eschatology. However, they are linked more closely than what many Evangelicals believe. This is addressed in several books including my own, Glorious Kingdom, where the major views of eschatology are presented. In this book, I argue for an optimistic view of the kingdom of God. Since communion is to be taken with 'remembering' until Jesus comes, we cannot neglect exploring this vital link when we partake of the Lord's Supper. Can it be that the term "Until he comes" is referring to a different arrival than a future, final coming? I am convinced it is not only possible but probable. Once the "He comes" is placed within its historical context and we take serious the words of Jesus, a different interpretation is warranted.

What did Jesus teach his disciples about his coming and when did he teach it? This is the best starting point. The question about "His coming" is found in Matthew 24, where the disciples ask about the events which will precede the destruction of the Jewish temple. The disciples had questions and one of them was "When will your coming take place?" This is not an isolated question from the context. They were not requesting a 'prophecy chart' for the ages, they wanted information about the timing of the Temple's destruction. If the question was to determine 'when' the temple was to be destroyed, why ask about his coming and the end of the age? In the minds of Jesus' followers, it was one question. If the Temple were to be destroyed it certainly would be the end of the Jewish age, which occurs with the 'Son of Man coming in his kingdom.'

Paul wrote:

I Corinthians 11:26

*For as often as you eat this bread and drink the cup, you proclaim the Lord's death until **he comes.***

Jesus said:

Matthew 10:23

*When they persecute you in one town, flee to the next, for truly, I say to you, you will not have gone through all the towns of Israel before the **Son of Man comes.***

There is no mystery as to who Paul was referring; the "He" was Jesus. When Jesus spoke of himself the term he used most was the "Son of Man."

Matthew 16:27-28

For the Son of Man is going to come with his angels in the glory of his Father, and then he will repay each person according to what he has done. ²⁸ Truly, I say to you, there are some standing here who will not taste death until they see the Son of Man coming in his kingdom.

The end of the age related to the arrival of the Messiah. Daniel called this the 'time of the end' (Dan.8:17, 12:4, 9). He did not call it the 'end of time.' First century followers of Jesus certainly saw the 'end of the age' and 'his coming' as related to his prophecy about the 'coming of the Son of Man' (Mat. 10:23). Is the 'coming of the kingdom' and 'until he comes' referring to the same event? If so, then this alters our standard view of communion and provides us with a solid foundation for seeing the Lords Table from a viewpoint of kingdom victory.

Jesus reminds his disciples that a future event in their life time was coming, which he called *"the Son of Man coming in his kingdom."* Jesus is telling his disciples he will come with angels, in the glory of his Father (which places this after the Ascension and Enthronement), and then, gives them a time table for his coming. As Jesus looked over the group he was speaking to, he probably saw different ages represented. He may have seen some young people in their teens or twenties, and then said, *"There are some standing here who will not taste death until they see the Son of Man coming in his kingdom."* When we connect this 'coming in his kingdom' with his coming to end the old covenant, linked to the destruction of the city and Temple, we then have an accurate timetable, about forty years, or one biblical generation. The majority who heard Jesus speak this prophecy would not be alive when this occurred, but some were.

Matthew 24:25-27

See, I have told you beforehand. [26] *So, if they say to you, 'Look, he is in the wilderness,' do not go out. If they say, 'Look, he is in the inner rooms,' do not believe it.* [27] *For as the lightning comes from the east and shines as far as the west, so will be the coming of the Son of Man.*

After Jesus warns his disciples about these future events, including the Great Tribulation (vs. 21) he gives information about his 'coming.' Since there will be false prophets and false Christs (Messiahs) during the next forty years, they are instructed "do not believe it." Then he foretells his coming in graphic terms of 'lighting', and continues in verse thirty-four telling 'when' he will come.

Matthew 24:34

Truly, I say to you, this generation will not pass away until all these things take place.

There can be no doubt Jesus was referring to an event which was to take place within a generation. He calls it a 'coming.' This is his words. The question begs us, is this what Apostle Paul was referring to when he said, *"proclaim the Lord's death until he comes?"*

What if the Apostle Paul wrote?

Proclaim the Lord's death until Jesus comes in his kingdom.

If Paul would have added the words "in his kingdom" then the answer should be obvious. Even though Paul only says, "until he comes", I am convinced it was the same event with the same time restriction as what Jesus spoke of. If this is true, then we must rework our standard understanding of communion. More than a slight 'reworking', it needs a radical overhaul.

This insight coincides with what Paul said *"For as often as you eat this bread and drink the cup, you proclaim the Lord's death until he comes* (I Cor.11:26). We should not allow this passage to be interpreted by modern authors who see it through a dispensational structure. Does this passage mean the final "Second Coming" as many ascribe it to, or can we go back to the words of Jesus and see how he used this terminology?

Another writer sets up the problem Jesus caused by not following the traditional structure. "Now what's the problem? The problem is that gospel account says something like this: after the third cup is drunk Jesus says, "I shall not drink again of the fruit of the vine until I am entering into the kingdom of God." And it says, "Then they sang the psalms." Every Jew who knows the liturgy would expect: and then they went ahead and said the grace and the blessing and had the fourth cup which climaxed and consummated the Passover. But no, the gospel account say they sang the psalms and went out into the night."[40]

Several Biblical scholars have stated their views of what it meant for Jesus to not drink wine with them again until he drinks it in the kingdom.

John Grill says, "The cup he had just drank of, was the last he should drink with them: he should drink no more wine at the Passover; he had kept the last, and which now of right was to cease; nor in the Lord's supper, for though that was to continue to his second coming, he should be no more present at it corporeally."[41]

Albert Barnes, "I am about to die. The design of all these types and shadows is about to be accomplished. This is the last time that I shall partake of them with you. Hereafter, when my Father's kingdom is established in heaven, we will partake together of the

---

[40] Dr. Scott Hahn, The Fourth Cup, Newman Apologetics Resource, zuserver2.star.ucl.ac.uk/~vgg/rc/aplgtc/hahn/m4/4cp.html
[41] John Grill, Gill's Exposition of the Entire Bible, Amazon Digital Services, Inc.

thing represented by these types and ceremonial observances - the blessings and triumphs of redemption."[42]

Both scholars take the passage to mean we will drink again with Jesus at the Second Coming or in heaven. This has been the stand Evangelical interpretation. But does it hold true when compared to other passages?

What if Paul was not thinking of our modern beliefs about the 'rapture' and 'Second Coming'; but had in mind the words of Jesus when he wrote "Until he comes?"

Let's review all the relevant passages.

Matthew 26:29

*I tell you I will not drink again of this fruit of the vine until that day when I drink it new with you in my **Father's kingdom**.*

Mark 13:25

*Truly, I say to you, I will not drink again of the fruit of the vine until that day when I drink it new in the **kingdom of God**.*

Luke 22:18

*For I tell you that from now on I will not drink of the fruit of the vine until the **kingdom of God comes**.*

I Corinthians 11:26

*For as often as you eat this bread and drink the cup, you proclaim the Lord's death **until he comes**.*

First, we must ask if Jesus needs to be with us physically to drink the fruit of the vine. If we answer yes, then, how can that be physically possible if we include the entire church? If we only

---

[42] Albert Barnes, Barnes Notes on the Whole Bible, Published by E4 Group, August 18, 2014

include the original disciples, then it loses meaning for the rest of us. Since the pouring out of the Holy Spirit, the Spirit of Christ is with and in his church.

Starting with Matthew's account we read Jesus will not drink of the fruit of the vine until he drinks it new in "My Fathers Kingdom." Both Mark and Luke write "The kingdom of God" instead of "My Fathers kingdom." Are the gospel writers speaking of two different things? Is the "Fathers kingdom" our abode in heaven, whereas the "kingdom of God' resides on earth. This is highly unlikely. All the authors are rewriting the account of what Jesus spoke. We allow for differences in words and sentence structure because of individual styles without compromising our commitment to divine inspiration. The gospel writers wrote of one kingdom only; the kingdom of God which the prophets linked with the coming of the Messiah.

Approaching the verses by Mark and Luke we are faced with a similar question. Both use the phrase 'kingdom of God' instead of "My Fathers kingdom." Is this kingdom, a future reality in heaven or a type of kingdom Premillennialism teaches?[43] Or do we agree with Jesus, who told us his 'coming in the kingdom' would happen within one generation?

As we look at Matthew 10:23 we must see it in light of the other passages about the coming of the 'Son of Man.' Jesus prophesied the coming of his kingdom within one generation. *When they persecute you in one town, flee to the next, for truly, I say to you, you will not have gone through all the towns of Israel before the* **Son of Man comes.** It must have been strange to hear Jesus talk about a future coming when he was standing in front of them. There was no real expectation of the death of their Messiah. Yet, Jesus in his teaching is preparing them for the events of not just the next several years (his death and resurrection) but the important

---

[43] Premillennialism is the belief that once Jesus returns to earth he then sets up his kingdom, which is a 1,000-year reign. Therefore, the Second Coming is before (pre) the kingdom, or millennium.

events over the next forty years. For our purposes, we need to note that in the words of Jesus, he is coming within one generation, not several thousand years in the future. He was coming within a generation.

When Jesus told his followers, there will be a coming of the 'Son of Man', we must not race to the conclusion he meant anything like the popular "Second Coming" teaching. This 'coming' was to occur within the first century. His coming was a 'spiritual' coming and therefore the feasting will also be a celebration in the Holy Spirit. We must not forget where the kingdom is located. *"For the kingdom of God is not a matter of eating and drinking but of righteousness and peace and joy in the Holy Spirit (Rom. 14:17)."* If we shorten the passage, we can read it *"For the kingdom of God is in the Holy Spirit."*

When Jesus took the third cup it represented the new covenant in his blood. Redemption had come! Salvation is at hand! Yet, beyond the cross and the arrival of the Holy Spirit, there was another great event in the life of the early church; the coming of Jesus in his kingdom. Once this happened, the church has full possession of the Messianic Kingdom. The signs of the old covenant are swept away and the body of Christ took its place as God's kingdom ambassadors in the earth. A study of Scripture and history leads to the conclusion that this took place during the Roman war on Jerusalem resulting with the complete destruction of the city and of the temple. The old ways are completely removed and it's time for a celebration.

Chapter 7

Wedding Parables

Jesus taught by telling stories and parables and one of his favorite themes was weddings. First century Jewish weddings had a prominent place in the lives of the people. In our first parable Jesus compares the kingdom of God to a wedding feast.

Matthew 22:1-10

And again Jesus spoke to them in parables, saying, [2] *"The* **kingdom of heaven may be compared to a king who gave a wedding feast for his son,** [3] *and sent his servants to call those who were invited to the wedding feast, but they would not come.* [4] *Again he sent other servants, saying, 'Tell those who are invited, "See, I have prepared my dinner, my oxen and my fat calves have been slaughtered, and everything is ready. Come to the wedding feast."'* [5] *But they paid no attention and went off, one to his farm, another to his business,* [6] *while the rest seized his servants, treated them shamefully, and killed them.* [7] *The king was angry, and he sent his troops and destroyed those murderers and burned their city.* [8] *Then he said to his servants, 'The wedding feast is ready, but those invited were not worthy.* [9] *Go therefore to the main roads and invite to the wedding feast as many as you find.'* [10] *And those servants went out into the roads and gathered all whom they found, both bad and good. So the wedding hall was filled with guests.*

For those holding dispensational views this passage has been used to teach how things will look at the end of history. Our misunderstanding of the words 'kingdom of heaven' may have contributed to this unfortunate interpretation. First, the phrase 'kingdom of heaven' is no different than 'kingdom of God.' As in the story of the prodigal son, to 'sin against heaven' is to 'sin against God.' The kingdom of heaven indicates that the origin of authority, of love, of grace, everything of God begins in 'God's space.' The kingdom of heaven comes from heaven but clearly is for the earth. Second, the term 'kingdom of God' is not a code word for heaven. The kingdom of God is God's activity on earth through his Son.

The story about a king giving a wedding for his son as a picture of Father God sending his Son to the people of Israel. The Prophets spoke of a coming Messiah for hundreds of years and now the time had arrived. Dispensational Christian author Jack Kelly agrees that the ten virgins represent Israel, but his conclusion concerning the timing is not consistent.

"The King represents God the Father, His Son our Lord Jesus. Invited guests who declined His invitation symbolize Israel's rejection of the Messiah and the servants He sent to invite them are the prophets. The city He destroyed is Jerusalem, and the wedding banquet is the Kingdom of Heaven. This puts the timing of the parable at the Second Coming."[44]

Why the jump to the Second Coming? It begins by a wrong interpretation of Matthew 24 as signs for the Second Coming. I covered Matthew 24 in my previous book <u>Glorious Kingdom</u> and my conclusion then and now is, Jesus in the Olivet Discourse gave his follower's signs for the tribulation and destruction of Jerusalem and its temple, which occurs within one generation. Therefore, a correct understanding of Matthew 24 is imperative for under-standing the New Testament and the purposes of God in his kingdom.

In this story of Jesus, he uses an invitation to a wedding as an illustration. Jesus came to his own and offered them the kingdom and they refused to receive it. First century Israel was invited into the kingdom and its feast. The words in the story that the king *'destroyed those murderers and burned their city'* has a haunting

---

[44] Jack Kelly, Rapture Ready, http://www.raptureready.com

feeling in light of what occurred. When Jerusalem was destroyed over one million lost their lives. In the parable, the city is burned before the feast began. This is a clear reference to the burning of Jerusalem in 70 A.D. The timing element is important. The kingdom wedding supper does not begin until after the city is burned.

Who is invited? Jesus first came to his own, the nation of Israel. Servants (his disciples) went out proclaiming the Messiah has come. We know by Scripture and history that Israel as a people rejected the invitation to enter the kingdom. Who will now attend the wedding? Who will enter the kingdom? In the story the servants go out and *"invite to the wedding feast as many as you find."* If Israel as a nation rejects the invitation of Jesus, then everyone else, that is Gentiles, are invited.

I love the beginning words of the parable. My translation would be simply, "The kingdom of God is like a feast." Coming into his kingdom is like being invited to a grand divine wedding feast. That is good news! Yet, it gets better. Unlike modern wedding feasts which last a day or up to a week in some cultures, the kingdom wedding feast never ends!

Matthew 21:42-45

Jesus said to them, "Have you never read in the Scriptures:

"'The stone that the builders rejected
has become the cornerstone
this was the Lord's doing,
and it is marvelous in our eyes'?

Therefore I tell you, the kingdom of God will be taken away from you and given to a people producing its fruits. And the one who falls on this stone will be broken to pieces; and when it falls on anyone, it will crush him." When the chief priests and the Pharisees heard his parables, they perceived that he was speaking about them.

Jesus is the stone and Israel rejected him. Now, this single stone is the cornerstone for a great structure, the kingdom of God. Therefore, the promises and possession of the kingdom of God, prophesied by the Hebrew Prophets, is taken away and given to another people. It is not that the complete 'bloodline' of Abraham is losing the kingdom, because for the first several decades the new people of God were all Jews. It was a matter of faith. The Jews who embraced Jesus came to the wedding feast. Then, the Gentiles were invited and many came.

Parable of the Ten Virgins

Matthew 25:1-10

Then the kingdom of heaven will be like ten virgins who took their lamps and went to meet the bridegroom.² Five of them were foolish, and five were wise. ³ For when the foolish took their lamps, they took no oil with them, ⁴ but the wise took flasks of oil with their lamps. ⁵ As the bridegroom was delayed, they all became drowsy and slept. ⁶ But at midnight there was a cry, 'Here is the bridegroom! Come out to meet him.' ⁷ Then all those virgins rose and trimmed their lamps. ⁸ And the foolish said to the wise, 'Give us some of your oil, for our lamps are going out.' ⁹ But the wise answered, saying, 'Since there will not be enough for us and for you, go rather to the dealers and buy for yourselves.' ¹⁰ And while they were going to buy, the bridegroom came, and those who were ready went in with him to the marriage feast, and the door was shut.

Jesus tells another parable. It is about ten virgins and a wedding. Is this the same wedding as in the previous parable? I believe it is. The Son of Man is the bridegroom and the ten virgins are Israel. If you were raised in a typical Evangelical church with dispensational eschatology, you heard this parable preached about 'missing the rapture.' In Pentecostal churches this parable was often used to teach if you are not 'baptized in the Holy Spirit' you will miss the rapture. This rush to a 'Second Coming' interpretation is seen by most who hold to a dispensational premillennial eschatology.

This parable is not about a future Second Coming. It is about his first coming to offer the kingdom to Israel. There is not several thousands of years between the destruction of the Jerusalem-and the wedding feast. The two are linked. One follows the other in a natural time line. And both are in the first century.

Matthew 24:29-30

Immediately after the tribulation of those days the sun will be darkened, and the moon will not give its light, and the stars will fall from heaven, and the powers of the heavens will be shaken. *[30] Then will appear in heaven the sign of the Son of Man, and then all the tribes of the earth will mourn, and they will see the Son of Man coming on the clouds of heaven with power and great glory.*

Once the city was destroyed, then the "Son of Man" came in his kingdom. And according to Jesus' own words will these things will be fulfilled within one generation. *"Truly, I say to you, this generation will not pass away until all these things take place.* *[35] Heaven and earth will pass away, but my words will not pass away* (Matthew 24:34).

The tribulation Jesus spoke of is the destruction of Jerusalem and its Temple. We are not waiting for this to happen; it already happened. When the Romans destroyed the temple and city in 70 A.D., it was the final sign that the old was finished and the new people of God were ready to be married. Let the wedding feast begin!

Theologian and Bible Teacher David Duncan:

"The marriage of Jesus and His Bride: Jesus came to Israel as their God, their Husband. The Husband who had made a covenant with Israel at Mt. Sinai had now come from heaven to earth to make a new covenant, a new marriage with Israel. Under the law, the legal way to end a marriage was for the husband to die, releasing the wife to marry another. We see this language mentioned in Romans 7:1-4.

Or do you not know, brothers—for I am speaking to those who know the law—that the law is binding on a person only as long as he lives? [2] *For a married woman is bound by law to her husband while he lives, but if her husband dies she is released from the law of marriage.* [3] *Accordingly, she will be called an adulteress if she lives with another man while her husband is alive. But if her husband dies, she is free from that law, and if she marries another man she is not an adulteress.* [4] *Likewise, my brothers, you also have died to the law through the body of Christ, so that you may belong to another, to him who has been raised from the dead, in order that we may bear fruit for God.*

Therefore, in this case, Jesus came as Israel's Messiah, as their Husband, to release her from the previous covenant, freeing her to marry anew. The goal was for Israel to embrace the cross and resurrection of Jesus, and enter the new covenant with their Husband, the resurrected Lord. Only a remnant, the believers of Israel, did this, and thus, this remnant carried the message of the kingdom to the rest of the world. This is the Israel of God.

This is the glory of the new covenant, a beautiful marriage. John, using prophetic symbolic language, speaks of this Bride as the New Jerusalem, a jeweled city with streets of pure gold, and gates of pearl. The names of the tribe of Israel on the gates, signifying that it's the remnant of Israel who opened the new covenant to the rest of the world. The names of the apostles of the Lord on the foundations under these gates, signifying the city of this new covenant marriage is built upon the teaching of the Lord's apostles, as well as, upon the new covenant prophecies found in our old testament...This marriage is the culmination of God's covenant journey with humanity which began in the garden of Eden, Adam and Eve being a type and shadow of this marriage relationship."[45]

Matthew 23:29-38

Woe to you, scribes and Pharisees, hypocrites! For you build the tombs of the prophets and decorate the monuments of the righteous, [30] saying, 'If we had lived in the days of our fathers, we would not have taken part with them in shedding the blood of the prophets.' [31] Thus you witness against yourselves that you are sons of those who murdered the prophets. [32] Fill up, then, the measure of your fathers. [33] You serpents, you brood of vipers, how are you to escape being sentenced to hell? [34] Therefore I send you prophets and wise men and scribes, some of whom you will kill and crucify, and some you will flog in your synagogues and persecute from town to town, [35] so that on you may come all the righteous blood shed on earth, from the blood of righteous Abel to the blood of Zechariah the son of Barachiah, whom you murdered between the sanctuary and the altar. [36] Truly, I say to you, all these things will come upon this generation.[37] "O Jerusalem, Jerusalem, the city that kills the prophets and stones those who are sent to it! How often would I have gathered your children together as a hen gathers her brood under her wings, and you were not willing! [38] See, your house is left to you desolate.

Jesus makes it clear that if the religious leaders of his day had lived in earlier times they would have joined those killing the prophets. To prove his point Jesus prophesies they will engage in the same behavior. Jesus said that prophets would be sent to them and they would kill them. As we know, this occurred in the early church. The prophets, beginning with John the Baptist and others were killed by the religious leaders. Therefore, when the book of Revelation talks about a city where the prophets are killed we should clearly understand; it is the city of Jerusalem being referred to.

---

[45] From a private message sent from David Duncan February 1st, 2016

These Scriptures help us determine the timing of the Marriage Supper of the Lamb. It follows the 'fall of Babylon' or the destruction of Jerusalem, which occurred in 70 A.D. First the tribulation, the killing of the prophets, the fall of the city and then the Wedding Feast begins! A common problem occurs when associating these events with a future time; when we all get to heaven. I do not see the 'marriage supper of the lamb' as a great dinner in heaven. We have seen the well-known painting of the great table in the sky, prepared and ready, waiting for those invited to arrive. This false understanding that after the 'rapture' the church sits down to the 'marriage feast' while the inhabitants of the worlds are being slaughtered by the millions, reveals a sad and misguided doctrine. We will not be floating in heaven, eating while God is pouring out his wrath on the world. The 'marriage feast of the lamb' has come. It is time to feast upon the goodness of God and celebrate all we have in the new covenant. "Whereas Western Christian art has traditionally associated heaven with clouds and harps, first century Jews thought of heaven as a time of feasting at Messiah's table."[46] Is it possible we have even misunderstood the basic nature of our eternal existence? Understanding the 'Lord's Table' is a good step in reclaiming the present reality of heaven.

Matthew 8:11-12

I tell you, many will come from east and west and recline at table with Abraham, Isaac, and Jacob in the kingdom of heaven, [12] while the sons of the kingdom will be thrown into the outer darkness. In that place there will be weeping and gnashing of teeth.

Notice how Jesus refers to the time of feasting at the Messiahs table with a time of judgment. This helps determine when we begin feasting and adds to our understanding of the Lord's Table from a kingdom perspective. In 70A.D. Jesus comes in his kingdom and takes the kingdom away from those not producing fruit (Matt. 21:43). This was first century unbelieving Israel. They were the

---

[46] Steve Atkerson, The Lord's Supper— A Holy Meal, www.ntrf.org

ones who by covenantal right possessed the kingdom until a new covenant was fully established in the earth.

Luke records a parable of Jesus about a wedding feast (Lk. 14:7-24). Jesus was teaching about preparing a feast and inviting "the poor, the crippled, the lame, and the blind, and you will be blessed." A person at the table then proclaimed, *"Blessed is everyone who will eat bread in the kingdom of God."*

We must refresh our thinking on how the Bible uses the term 'kingdom of God.' Those living in the first century, Jews and Christians alike, would not jump to the conclusion many make today, that 'kingdom' is a code word for heaven. It was not about going to heaven, but about experiencing the promises of God in the age of the Messiah. To eat bread in the kingdom was to enjoy the blessings of the Messiah.

The concept of 'bread' and the 'coming kingdom' is part of how Jesus taught his disciples to pray. "Your kingdom come. Give us each day our daily bread (Lk. 11:2-3)." "The Greek underlying Luke 11:3 is difficult to translate. Literally, it reads something akin to, "the bread of us belonging to the coming day give us today" (the NASV marginal note reads, "bread for the coming day").[47]

Followers of Jesus were to eat the bread of a day yet to come. This was before the cross, before the resurrection and enthronement and before the "day" of the coming of the son of man in his kingdom (Matt. 10:23, 16:27-28). The New Testament was written when two ages occupied the same space. The first generation of Christians lived while the old covenant was being practiced in the Temple. The day of the Messiah arrived with the birth of Jesus and yet it was not until the Temple and Jerusalem were destroyed that the fullness of the kingdom manifested itself on earth. Even though early church members were born again and entered the kingdom,

---

[47] Ibid.

there was yet a future and greater manifestation of the kingdom with the "coming of the son of man."

When the Temple came down, the feasting began! It was the final sign that God's kingdom had come and the people of Jesus had entered a new age.

Chapter 8

The Mystery of the Fourth Cup

Luke 22:18

For I tell you that from now on I will not drink of the fruit of the vine until the kingdom of God comes.

Mark 14:25

Truly, I say to you, I will not drink again of the fruit of the vine until that day when I drink it new in the kingdom of God.

Even though it is repetitious we must reinforce in our minds that the expression 'kingdom of God' is not a code phrase for heaven. Christians in the first century would find this confusing. For them kingdom language was all about what God through the Messiah was doing in their lives on the earth. They saw that the kingdom is from heaven but is manifest on the earth. When Jesus spoke of drinking the 'fruit of the vine' with them in the kingdom, it would have been expected to happen within their life time, or at least in their children's life. Why? Because Jesus told them about a 'coming' within one generation. The drinking of the fourth cup would be a time of celebration on earth, when his followers realized Jesus as the "Son of Man" has come in his kingdom.

We now come to the Lord's Table with the full awareness that Jesus is king. We commune with him as we drink the fourth cup. We commune with each other in our celebration of the new covenant. What does the fourth cup represent? Why is it different than the third cup and how should that alter our approach to the Lord's Table? These questions can be answered by examining the words of Jesus when he said, *"I will drink it new in the kingdom of God."*

If Jesus followed the standard guidelines of faithful Jews, then, why did he alter the service? Jesus never finished the service, he never drank the fourth cup. Everything seems similar to the old patterns, that is, until he explained the meaning of the third cup. When he declared, the cup was the new covenant in his blood, the Jewish tradition was eternally changed, and the world would never be the same. Then, after ascribing to the third cup a radical new understanding, Jesus refused the final cup, waiting for the kingdom of God. Herein lies the mystery. It seems the completion of this new way of celebrating Passover was on hold for a short time, that is, until the 'Son of Man' comes in his kingdom. Jesus went from the third cup to the final hymn, by-passing the fourth one.

What was the fourth cup? What does it symbolize? Why did Jesus not drink it during his Passover meal with his disciples? What does "*I will drink it new in the kingdom of God*" mean?

One view is that Jesus drank the 'fourth cup' while on the cross. The reason I do see not see the cross as fulfilling his promise to "Drink it anew in the kingdom of God" is that this cup is in direct relationship to the coming of the kingdom. Yes, the cross established the victory of God over all his enemies. Without the cross, there is no kingdom. Yet, the door into something is not the final destination. We have Jesus' words about the coming of the kingdom and he clearly states when the "Son of Man" comes. Jesus provides us with a time reference as to when this 'coming' will occurs. In Matthew 24:29-30, the coming of the "Son of Man" is immediately after the tribulation. This tribulation is when Jerusalem and the temple were destroyed. The forty-two months prior to the year 70 A.D. is when the 'Great Tribulation' took place. Therefore, although we can appreciate the thought of Jesus receiving a drink of wine before his death, I see a greater fulfillment coming.

Let's review the four cups and expand on the last. According to Mike Ratliff the four Passover cups represented four aspects of God's working with Israel.

1. The Cup of Sanctification – based on God's statement, "I will bring you out from under the burdens of the Egyptians"
2. The Cup of Judgment or Deliverance- based on God's statement, "I will deliver you from slavery to them"
3. The Cup of Redemption – based on God's statement, "I will redeem you with an outstretched arm"
4. The Cup of Praise or Restoration – based on God's statement, "I will take you to be my people, and I will be your God"[48]

Most scholars have similar wording, although some add the 'consummation of the kingdom' as part of the fourth cup. They believe that is why Jesus never partook of it. As we have seen, it is common to teach the last cup being linked to the second coming of Christ. Yet, when we see that the coming of the "Son of Man in his kingdom" has very strict time limits it becomes problematic to place it far into the future. If we view this coming in the kingdom as the events of 70A.D., then it begins to make sense.

David Brickner from the ministry of Jews for Jesus gives us a similar explanation for the four cups. "Each time the cup is filled, it has a different name. Opinions vary as to what certain cups actually symbolize. Most agree that the first cup is the *Kiddush*, which means sanctification. With this cup, we begin the Passover Seder. The second cup is called the cup of plagues. The third cup is referred to as either the cup of redemption or the cup of blessing. The fourth cup is often called *hallel* which means praise.[49]"

God established a new people under a 'new covenant.' The first covenant was broken; its visible end was approaching fast. The first covenant was not corrected or altered and then established again by the coming of Jesus. The new covenant is totally new. What was continuous was the people; a remnant of Israel was the first to enter God's new arrangement. Now being connected to

---

[48] Mike Ratliff, The four cups of wine of Passover, www.mikeratliff@wordpress.com
[49] David Brickner, The Mystery of the Passover Cup, 2002, http://www.jewsforjesus.org

Jesus by being born from above is the only means for a relationship with God. The people of the Messiah will be "my people." Drinking the fourth cup is a time of praise for the new people of God, the body of Christ.

Even after the cross and resurrection, there was an event yet to occur, and Jesus refers to it as his coming. What was so essential about the final cup of the celebration? And why the delay? The gap between the third and fourth cup was because the age of transition was at hand. Even though at the cross the curtain of the temple was torn in two allowing free access to the Father, the visible structure of the old covenant was standing. If the old temple stood, many would think the old covenant remained God's method for correct worship. In addition, beyond the signs of the old covenant was the problem of the 'afflictions' upon Christians by the Jews. Paul made this clear in his letter to the believers in Thessaloniki.

I Thessalonians 2:14-16

And we also thank God constantly for this, that when you received the word of God, which you heard from us, you accepted it not as the word of men but as what it really is, the word of God, which is at work in you believers. [14] For you, brothers, became imitators of the churches of God in Christ Jesus that are in Judea. For you suffered the same things from your own countrymen as they did from the Jews, [15] who killed both the Lord Jesus and the prophets, and drove us out, and displease God and oppose all mankind [16] by hindering us from speaking to the Gentiles that they might be saved—so as always to fill up the measure of their sins. But wrath has come upon them at last!

Apostle Paul was a Jew. He loved and prayed for his own people. Yet, he knew they were hindering the gospel and by so doing were filling up the *measure of their sins* which would result in judgment. The separation of unbelieving Jews from the Christian community occurred when the "Son of Man" came and executed judgment on old Israel. This ended the visible signs of the old covenant and stopped the vicious afflictions from the Jews. As one covenant ended another came into its fullness. When the "Son of Man" came in judgment upon apostate Israel he also came to celebrate his marriage to the bride; the church. It is now time for the "Marriage Supper of the Lamb."

The Marriage Super of the Lamb

When did Jesus drink the fourth cup? We know the final cup was to be taken in close connection to the coming of the kingdom. Therefore, it is not unreasonable at all, in fact, it is reasonable to conclude the drinking of the fourth cup was during the Marriage Supper of the Lamb. This is the feast for the wedding between Christ and his wife; the church.

In Revelation chapter nineteen we have the passage where John says, *"The marriage of the Lamb has come."* Right before this declaration John wrote, *"Fallen, fallen is Babylon the great* (Rev. 18:2)! Do we know what city he is referring to? A major clue is remembering what Jesus said about the killing of the prophets. When we understand Matthew 23, we will make sense of chapter 24, and when that becomes clear, the whole book of Revelation is much easier to understand.

Since communion is our topic, a complete review of John's book is outside of the scope of this work. Yet, making a connection is vital to seeing how the Lord's Table is celebrated in the new covenant. Revelation nineteen cannot be separated from the previous subject in chapters 13-18. When we begin reading the verses in chapter nineteen it is the conclusion and finality of the judgments of God upon apostate Israel.

David S. Clark, in his book The Message from Patmos makes this clear.

"This chapter stands in the closest connection with the chapters preceding. We have seen the vials of judgment poured out open the beast and seat of the beast...Now in the opening of the nineteenth chapter we have the rejoicing of heaven over the judgment of the harlot city. A great voice of much people in heaven says: "'Hallelujah! Salvation and glory and power belong to our God, for his judgments are true and just; for he has judged the great prostitute who corrupted the earth with her immorality, and has avenged on her the blood of his servants.'"[50]

Revelation 19:6-8

Then I heard what seemed to be the voice of a great multitude, like the roar of many waters and like the sound of mighty peals of thunder, crying out,

"Hallelujah!
For the Lord our God
  the Almighty reigns.
[7] *Let us rejoice and exult*
  and give him the glory,
*for the **marriage of the Lamb has come,***
  and his Bride has made herself ready;
[8] *it was granted her to clothe herself*
  with fine linen, bright and pure"—for the fine linen is the
righteous deeds of the saints.

This is the feast for the wedding between Christ and his wife; the church. The timing is the same as "The Son of Man coming in his Kingdom", which was at the conclusion of the great tribulation; 70 A.D. Even though this is not the 'normal' interpretation, it is not a novel one or an unwarranted one.

The 'Fourth Cup' is now available. Jesus is inviting us to his heavenly table, and this is what we celebrate during communion.

---

[50] David S. Clark, The Message from Patmos, Baker Book House, Grand Rapids, Michigan, 1989, p. 117

The Mystery of the Fourth Cup is solved. We drink the final cup of wine, the new covenant wine at the Marriage Supper of the Lamp. The best news is we keep drinking, we keep eating. Every Sunday the church meets to worship and the final aspect of our worship is celebrating the life we have with Jesus by eating at his table. This is not an event that only occurs in history. Similar to the pouring out of the Holy Spirit on the day of Pentecost, it was a one-time historical event, yet the Spirit continues to be poured out throughout all generations. So is the Marriage Supper of the Lamb continued through the ages.

Marriage and Feasting

"In biblical times, the notion of a wedding without a banquet was unthinkable. So intertwined were the ideas marriage and feast that one of the definitions of the Greek word for wedding (gamos) is actually "wedding feast." The connection may be seen in the meaning of the root (gam) which is "to join." To wed is to join together. But, in biblical times, sharing a table was also a means of intimate fellowship. Covenant meals indicated that two parties were now joined together in a new relational context. Marriage is a covenant (Mal. 2:14). So, feasting at a wedding was an integral component of the marriage event."[51]

A marriage today can last 50-80 years at best. The marriage between Christ and his bride is forever. It is essential that we understand the biblical connection between the marriage and the celebration of the marriage.

The Lord's Table-The Heart of Worship

David Chilton wrote a classic commentary on the book of Revelation. He wrote:

---

[51] Stan McGehee Jr, Marriage Supper of the Lamb, http://lwcchurch.org/newsletter/April 2011/marriagesupper.php

"It should go without saying (but, unfortunately, it cannot), that the Eucharist is the center of Christian worship; the Eucharist is what we are commanded to do when we come together on the Lord's Day. Everything else is secondary."[52]

Secondary things are important. Preaching is important. The church must be instructed. Singing and praise is important. Prayer is important. Yet, none of these were meant to replace partaking of the Lord's Table.

When we receive communion, we are participating in the Marriage Supper of the Lamb. We celebrate our oneness with our Lord. We honor our unity with each other. We exult the Kingship of Jesus. We advance the kingdom every time we eat at the Lord's Table. Why would any Pastor or team of elders not want to receive communion every week?

David Chilton: "The greatest privilege of the Church is her weekly participation in the Eucharistic meal, the Marriage Supper of the Lamb."[53]

I dream of a day when evangelicals believe this. Talk about revival, work toward transformation, strategize about building a kingdom/new covenant church. Yet, if we forsake the Lord's Table and demote it to something less than the heart of worship, then, whatever we gain in our pursuits will be incomparable to what we could have walked in.

As God is transforming his church with revelation of the kingdom and the new covenant, let's pursue the same with communion. Let's restore the Table of the Lord to its proper place in our Sunday services. Let us move from a 'mere remembering' to experiencing the real presence of Christ. Let us move away from conducting a corporate funeral service to celebrating the marriage of Christ and his church. Let us be the church that demonstrates to

---

[52] David Chilton, The Days of Vengeance, Dominion Press, Ft. Worth, Texas, 1987, p. 476
[53] Ibid.

the world that the kingdom of God has come as we drink and celebrate with Jesus the fourth cup.

Chapter 9

Practical Concerns

How did the early church view communion? Was it peripheral or central to their worship? Did they kneel or stand? Did they drink grape juice and eat crackers or use wine and bread? Were children allowed to partake or was it only a 'grown-up' thing? How often was it served? Who can serve the Lord's Table? There are many questions Christians have concerning the Lord's Table.

German theologian Jürgen Moltmann gives us his six imperatives concerning the Lord's Table.

1. Communion must be central to the Christian community, must be integrated into the heart of the worship service (not tacked on at the end), and must be celebrated with bread and wine.
2. The table must be open to those of varying theological views.
3. Baptism and confirmation must not be prerequisites for the fellowship of the table.
4. Everyone who follows Christ is qualified to administer the sacrament, and everyone is called upon to offer and distribute the elements.
5. Not only should the person performing the liturgy face the congregation, but the entire worship space should, if possible, be redesigned to a "'common room' in which the participants can see and talk to one another.'"
6. Communion should always be followed by "a common meal, and the proclamation of the gospel by a common

discussion of people's real needs and the specific tasks of Christian mission."[54]

Of Moltmann's six points I agree with all of them, even if number five and six are impractical. He points us to the importance of the Lord's Table and gives us direction for its practical application. How would the average communion service change if all these points were enacted? If we only took the first point seriously, 'Communion must be central to the Christian community' it would bring radical change to most churches. Let's be honest. If a church does not take communion every Sunday, it does not consider it central to their worship.

I realize there are strong opinions on all these matters and churches have split over their demand to 'correctly do communion.' Therefore, we proceed with caution but remain convinced once we understand more fully the revelation of the fourth cup the practical matters will not be matters for division but a celebration of unity.

Who Can Serve Communion?

Can only ordained ministers officiate the Lord's Table? Who is qualified to conduct the service? I find it interesting in churches which demand only ordained ministries serve the Lord's Table that they serve the people the elements, bread and wine, and then the people pass elements one to another. Maybe this is why in Roman Catholic and Eastern Orthodox Churches people come forward and receive directly from the Priest.

If the New Testament is our church book of order for conducting the communion service, then, there is nothing clearly stated about who can or cannot serve communion. The New Testament churches had elders and leaders, so we can conclude they were the 'overseers' of communion. Yet, we read about people 'breaking

---

[54] Jürgen Moltmann, The Church in the Power of the Spirit-A Contribution to Messianic Ecclesiology, First Fortress Press, 1993, p. 259-60.

break' on a regular basis in their homes. Was there an elder there in all cases? We cannot be sure, most likely not. It seems 'receiving' the Lord's Table is more important than the person leading the service.

Moltmann, in his fourth point addresses this. He states, "Everyone who follows Christ is qualified to administer the sacrament." Yet, this is seldom done. Almost without exception the Pastor leads the communion service. Even when my theological convictions convince me 'all believers' can serve communion, we must include common sense in addition to our theology. First, I assume Pastors are believers, so they can lead the communion service. Second, the Bible teaches the church is governed by leaders and therefore it seems logical they would serve the communion. Third, we would not desire people who are not known and have not demonstrated a consistent faith to administer the communion. Fourth, having the Pastor, or better, a team of Pastors/Elders-conduct the communion service is a way of demonstrating caring and responsible leadership. Therefore, even if 'all believers' can serve communion, I do not recommend waging war over the issue. The best place to implement the policy of 'all believers' would be in home meetings. This will strengthen the concept of the 'priesthood of all believers' and demonstrate the unity of the body of Christ.

What about Children?

Should children be allowed to participate in the Lord's Table? I find no clear conviction among churches, especially among the evangelical churches. Denominations often have rules spelled out in their 'Book of Order' or statement of belief but for churches outside the denominational world, there are a variety of rules, often unwritten, developed through years of tradition.

Rules for Excluding Children from Communion

Salvation

The first and primary rule in many churches is the 'rule of salvation.' We are told, children must be 'born again' before receiving communion. This seems logical. We would not want to share our spiritual table with a bunch of heathen. Yet, we encourage our children to pray, worship and 'pretend' to be Christians in every other way, but "Do not take communion." Again, what is communion and what does it represent? If the only reason is to 'remember' the cross, then babies and small children cannot benefit. If it is experiencing the 'real' presence of Christ in the community of faith, then, yes, everyone can benefit. If it is a 'celebration' of our union with Christ and of his body (the church), then again, everyone can benefit. Once we change our minds about the nature and purpose of communion then many of these issues lose their importance. A typical warning goes like this, "If you're a parent and you're not sure if your child is saved, don't let them take communion. This can avoid giving a false-assurance of salvation, and may even provoke good questions from your child."[55]

This 'rule' depends upon how we think children come to salvation. Must they say a certain prayer? Must they walk the aisle to the front of the church? It is not as simple as we may think. It is common for a child to grow in their faith and understanding. They may say 'the prayer' in a Sunday school class at seven, and then at ten, walk the aisle, and then again at a teen summer camp, get saved again. When should they begin taking communion? The 'rule of salvation' does not work well for children of believing parents.

---

[55] Scot Crook, Why Should a person be water-baptized before taking communion, http://crossgrace.org

Baptism

The second common rule is that partaking of the communion must follow baptism. Even though this rule also excludes all 'unbaptized believers,' it is children who receive the brunt of the rule. It is simple. No baptism-no communion.

Here is an example of how a pastor in the Southern Baptist denomination explains the rules of communion.

"Confession of faith unambiguously recognizes that biblical baptism is prerequisite to participation in the Lord's Supper." Southern Baptists' view of biblical baptism entails a profession of faith and full immersion in water in the name of the Trinity. Celebrating the Lord's Supper involves commemorating Christ's death and resurrection and also communing with the whole body of Christian believers. Southern Baptists believe only those who have publicly entered this community through believer's baptism may participate in communion."[56]

If we hold to the rule that 'baptism precedes communion', we need to consider the mode of baptism. Would a Baptist or Pentecostal Church allow a member of the Anglican Church, like N.T. Wright, to participate in communion with them? Since the Anglican Church practices 'infant baptism' and not 'believers' baptism' like most evangelicals, we can assume that only those baptized after conversion and by full immersion would be invited to the communion table. Rules can quickly become very exclusive. If we hold to this rule ("if you are not baptized by immersion, then, you cannot receive communion") then we must conclude the majority of our great Christian heroes throughout the ages would have been barred from celebrating communion.

I like the United Methodist Church statement on communion. Their 'Book of Worship' explains, "All who intend to

---

[56] Wes Kenney, Trinity Baptist Church, Valliant, Oklahoma, hppt://people.opposingviews.com/southern-baptist

lead a Christian life, together with their children, are invited to receive the bread and cup."[57]

Intellectual Qualifications

A third common rule is that a person must have the intellectual ability to 'understand communion.' Even though I have never seen an IQ test given to adults, we cannot allow ignorant children to partake in something they do not understand. At first glance this may seem reasonable. Yet, this rule would also rule out adults who are illiterate, those with mental disabilities and those with limited education. Applying this rule to children, without considering others with 'intellectual limits', is poor practice and bad theology.

Most local churches have rules, but most of these 'rules' are unofficial and not written. However, they are strictly enforced by the culture of the church. The message is clear; communion is for adults only. Children, including teenagers are not allowed to participate. I've asked several Pastors over the years why such a policy exists. The common answer goes like this, 'We want to insure people understand the communion before receiving it." If this is our reason, it is not reasonable. I'm not talking just about babies and small children. I've seen older teenagers (the same ones leading worship) pass the elements every time communion is served. The same argument is used "teens cannot understand 'doctrine.' We send them to advanced classes in High School, where they study and master subjects many adults in church would find difficult, yet, we are not sure if they can understand communion. Do we want to place an 'intellectual minimum' for those invited to partake? And if we do, what about those who fail?

The common evangelical rule is no. No children allowed. Why? Because they do not understand. Really? Then, what about the multitudes of illiterate people in third world countries who

---

[57] United Methodist Church, Can Children take Communion, htpp://www.umc.org

regularly take communion? Can they provide the pastor or elders a concise theology of communion? Can the average Western Christian make a biblical statement about it? If knowledge is the door, then, we had better improve our teaching. In the real church world, this is an excuse and pat answer for parents questioning if their children can receive communion.

Pedo-communion is the theological term for children being allowed to take communion. The academic argument can be complicated, but here are a few guidelines which should be helpful. We must take several issues seriously. First, the children of Christians should be considered part of the 'covenant community' until they prove otherwise. This means they do not have to 'prove a salvation experience', yet it does means we expect them to. If the nourishment of the Lord's Table is only for the strong and the weak are excluded, then, are we robbing them opportunities for growth? We must view the Table of the Lord, not as an exclusive club for members only, but as God's loving grace reaching out to all. God invites us to experience the life of his son, he encourages us to partake and see how Jesus can make a difference.

Rule of Speaking in Tongues

As a missionary in Bulgaria I learned of yet another rule, unwritten as it was, to forbid children from the Lord's Table. In Pentecostal churches, I noticed children and teens rarely take communion. I asked different Pastors and leaders and never got a straight answer, except the common ones already discussed. After several years of watching and observing, the answer of this mystery became clear. One Sunday morning a teenager came up front and testified about being baptized in the Holy Spirit and 'speaking in tongues.' The following Sunday was communion time. I was on the same row as this teenager and her mother. When the communion plate came the teenager, as always, passed it on. Her mother gave her a gentle nudge, meaning, 'take the communion.' The light came on! Receiving communion was not about, 'personal sin' or 'intellectual understanding.' The dividing line was simple. If you speak in tongues, you are in, if you do not, you are out. Those outside of a traditional Pentecostal church may find this 'unwritten' rule outrageous, yet, other denominations have their own rules which are just as bizarre.

Matthew Henry says communion is "food for the soul."[58] I wish evangelicals believed it. We are so focused in having 'solemn memories' we neglect to realize we are partaking in a spiritual meal. The meal we receive is the finest spiritual cuisine available. Jesus does not serve his church junk food. What is this "food for the soul?" It is the presence of Jesus. He feeds us with his presence. Why are we starving our children?

What day should we receive Communion?

"On the first day of the week, when we were gathered together to break bread (Acts 20:7)." The church in the book of Acts met regularly on Sundays. Why did they meet? Did they sing? Yes. Did they pray? Yes. Was there teaching? Yes. Was there participation from the congregation? Yes. Were gifts of the Holy Spirit manifested? Yes. We know these things occurred from other New Testament writings. Yet, when Luke mentioned their gathering on the first day of the week, it was to "break bread." This is communion. Receiving the Lord's Supper was not an option for the early church, it was a regular part of their Sunday worship. To meet on Sundays for worship and not receive communion was not in the mindset of Apostles and Elders of the early church. This was more than 'one additional' element of their worship; it was their reason for gathering. If this has any truth, then most evangelicals are far removed from the pattern we see in Scripture and in the early church. If we desire to be an 'apostolic church', then restoring the Lord's Table is a good place to start. It seems our biggest fear as evangelicals is not becoming overly traditional or coming close to a 'liturgy.' Maybe a true 'Spirit-

---

[58] Matthew Henry, Matthew Henry's Concise Commentary, Christian Classics Ethereal Library, 2010

filled' liturgy for Pentecostals and Charismatics is needed. I would say in this regard we have much to learn.

Wine or Grape Juice?

The fact we even have this debate should be a concern. The New Testament is clear and simple; they broke bread and drank wine. The problem lies in our current religious culture, not any duplicity found in Scripture. I have heard minister's claim serving wine for communion would be a sin and then another exhorting on how serving grape juice would be a sin. People will be upset no matter which side you support. Can you imagine the 'talk' if the average American Pastor substituted wine for the normal grape juice? And the opposite is true, in most countries Christians would find it offensive if grape juice replaced wine. Yet, in many American evangelical churches, even giving an option of wine would be a huge challenge. Pastors and leaders will need the Wisdom of Solomon to sort this out, but as with most areas, burying our heads in the sand is not the answer.

How do we take Communion?

Once we figure out the meaning of communion and decide to take it more often, how do we proceed?

Separate Cups and Pre-Broken Bread

From my experience, most churches practice one method for receiving communion. The pastor or elders pass a plate of 'communion wafers' and we take one and hold it. Then a large tray of individual glasses of grape juice (or wine if outside the United States) comes down the aisle. Once everyone is served and has the elements in hand, the Pastor says a few words, reads a Scripture, and prays. Then we eat the bread and drink the juice. Yet, this is only one way to receive communion.

Common Cup

Have you received communion using a common cup? For at least fifteen years I was in churches that used a 'common cup.' And the cup was filled with wine not grape juice. No one complained; no one refused. Finally, a few began to question the use of wine and also the use of a common cup. The church leaders were told, "It is not safe, and we might get sued if someone gets sick or catches a disease." Finally, as the Pastor, along with the elders, we began serving wine and grape juice in individual glasses and we moved forward. I still like the concept and symbolism of the common cup. Yet, realistically it is difficult to convince others, so most churches use individual glasses.

Intinction Method

There is another way of communion, a very old method, of using a common cup without mustering the fears of people, it is called the Intinction method. You begin by pouring the wine into a common cup. Then from a single loaf of bread, a piece is broken. This keeps the symbolism of the church being 'one community.' Then people come forward, take a piece of bread, and dip it into the wine and eat it. This method has several advantages. First, a large number of people can be served quickly because there can be several cups spread across the church. Second, the common cup and single loaf is a visible sign of our unity and participation in the body of Christ. Third, it reassures those fearful of drinking out of a common cup. It does have one disadvantage and that is the church does not partake at the same time. Yet, for everything it offers, it is a great method for receiving communion.

We must not create rules where Scripture is unclear. We know they shared the Lord's Table every Sunday. We know they took it often in homes. What we do not know is the exact method they used. Therefore, we should choose the best method that's fits our local congregation and focus on the meaning rather than the method.

Chapter 10

What is Kingdom Communion?

The communion service has taken on its own identity as a separate 'worship service.' Those things we deem not that important are the first things we put off for another day. In the church the 'unimportance' is reinforced by its infrequent use. By delegating the 'communion service' to a monthly, quarterly or 'whenever we feel like it', we have consciously or unconsciously made a bold statement. This statement is, "We view our normal worship service as separate from taking communion." We therefore have a 'normal worship' and then we have a 'special worship', which is eating at the Lord's Table. This is a tragedy for the church. Nothing could be further from the teaching and experience of the early church.

A flawed view of worship leads to a dismissal of the communion. We may not totally dismiss it, but by removing it from the weekly worship service we deem it less important. Singing is more important; we must sing every Sunday. Praise is more important. Prayer is more important. Receiving an offering is more important. Even the giving of announcements is done weekly. But not eating from the Lords Table!

Therefore, we have lowered its value in sight of the congregation.

It is time for the church to renew the place of communion to its rightful prominence. Let's take it off the 'back burner' and set it front and center in our weekly worship. Let the people feast on the Lord; and thus, build stability in the congregation, adding a piece of objectivity to our worship.

I have one more thought to be added to everything said about communion. It is the very act of partaking of communion which is important. Preaching about communion is not communion. The action of God's people coming to the Lord's Table is the means of God's grace and presence being once again activated in the Church. N.T. Wright says, "The bread-breaking meal, the Jesus feast, announces to the forces of evil like a public decree read out by a herald in the marketplace that Jesus is Lord, that he has faced the powers of sin and death and beaten them, and that he has been raised again to launch the new world in which death itself will have no authority."[59] These results of announcing the victory of Jesus is accomplished through receiving communion, not just taking about it.

Summary of Kingdom Communion

1. **Kingdom Communion is coming to the Lord's Table with a deep revelation of the King.**
2. **Kingdom Communion is moving from a death focused service to a time of celebration.**
3. **Kingdom Communion invites the family of God, including children, to partake of the real presence of Jesus, which is uniquely experienced at his Table.**
4. **Kingdom Communion is an important part of our Sunday Service, as vital as preaching, singing, prayer and worship.**
5. **Kingdom Communion is the renewing of the new covenant.**
6. **Kingdom Communion is communing with each other, fellowshipping with the body of Christ.**
7. **Kingdom Communion is a means of grace, Jesus strengthening and nourishing his church.**
8. **Kingdom Communion is receiving the cup of blessing God has for his family.**
9. **Kingdom Communion celebrates the coming of the Kingdom of God.**

---

[59] N.T. Wright, The Day the Revolution Began, Harper Collins, New York, New York, 2016, p. 380

10. Kingdom Communion is drinking the 'fourth cup' with Jesus in celebration of our union in marriage.
11. Kingdom Communion is one of the means God uses to bring healing and health to his people.
12. Kingdom Communion is the heart of worship.

A Vision for a Renewed Communion.

One day believers across the land will wake on Sunday morning eagerly anticipating coming to church. Even though every day is lived for Jesus, Sunday, the Lord's Day is special. It is the day we gather for worship, teaching and fellowshipping around the Table of the Lord. We sing and worship. Prayers are offered. Elders come and bless the bread and wine. The atmosphere is filled with love, acceptance and especially the presence of God. The glass is raised, "To the King," and everyone responds, "To the King." Family by family pass by the elders to receive the Lord's Supper. Leaders are nearby for those wanting special prayer and ministry. Hugs are plentiful. So are tears. Not in grief or sadness, but in overwhelming joy of Jesus and his new covenant. Music of celebration penetrates the room. Some kneel, others dance, and some sit quietly. Finally, all are served. Everyone stands. Together we sing of our wonderful Lord and King. We have renewed once again the new covenant. It never gets old; never!

Books by Stan Newton

Glorious Kingdom

A Handbook of Partial Preterist Eschatology

Glorious Kingdom is a comprehensive book on eschatology; kingdom eschatology. In this book, Stan Newton takes on dispensational eschatology, which is the position of many evangelicals and lays a foundation from Scripture for a different view. Glorious Kingdom covers all major aspects of eschatology with special emphasis on interpreting the prophetic New Testament passages from the viewpoint of the kingdom of God. The kingdom was established by Jesus in the first century. This book will help those seeking biblical answers to tough questions on eschatology.

Glorious Covenant

Our Journey Toward Better Covenant Theology

God is a God of covenants. Christians have a covenant. With these two basic foundations Stan Newton compares contemporary views of covenant. He examines Dispensationalism, Covenant Theology, and New Covenant Theology. Glorious Covenant finds the fault lines of each position and then through Scriptural discovery argues for a fourth view; Better Covenant Theology. Sadly, many Christians are only vaguely aware of this glorious covenant. How followers of Jesus understand covenant is extremely important and Glorious Covenant removes the confusion and presents a clear view of the New Covenant we have in Christ.

Breakfast at Tel Aviv

A Conversation about Israel

Theological Fiction

Shane recently graduated from a Pentecostal Bible school. His future was secure within his denomination except one very large adjustment; his changed his theology. After finishing seminary, he moves back near his hometown church and former pastor to begin his ministry. Pastor George is waiting for answers. Over coffee the question is asked, "Shane, you have not abandoned Israel, have you?"

Breakfast in Tel-Aviv is the story of Pastor Shane and Pastor George as they share their positions on Israel. Emotions are high as they regularly discuss their views. Their discussions lead to a trip to Israel and over breakfast all is resolved; or is it?

Kingdom Missions

The Ministry of Stan and Virginia Newton

We are singularly focused on teaching and demonstrating the Gospel of the Kingdom as taught in Stan's book, <u>Glorious Kingdom</u>. Through Seminars/Bible Schools/Churches we present the view of Christ's present and advancing Kingdom. We need your help in taking this message to the nations. You can E-mail us at <u>svnewton@hotmail.com</u> or become a friend on Facebook. To send letters or financial gifts please mail to Kingdom Missions-PO Box 948, Seattle, WA 98111. Also, give using PayPal. E-Mail for PayPal is <u>stannewton@live.com</u>.

Stan is available for speaking engagements in your church; please E-mail us. He also does Kingdom Seminars and can assist pastors and churches making the transition from being a Dispensational thinking church to a Victorious Kingdom/New Covenant one.

CPSIA information can be obtained
at www.ICGtesting.com
Printed in the USA
LVOW13s0337220617

538847LV00025B/653/P